PINSTRIPING 2 Masters

PINSTRIPING
2 Masters

More Techniques, Tricks, and Special F/X for Laying Down the Line

Published by Nikko Press, A Subsidiary of Airbrush Action, Inc.

Executive Publisher & Editor: Cliff Stieglitz
Technical Editor: Gary Jenson
Copy Editor: Cliff Stieglitz
Book Design: Chris Hughes
Production Designer: Brian Woodruff

Special Thanks to Gary Jenson for policing the integrity
of the information contained in this book.

First published in the United States of America by:
Nikko Press, A Subsidiary of Airbrush Action, Inc.
P.O. Box 438
Allenwood, NJ 08720
Tel: (732) 223-7878
Fax: (732) 223-2855

E-mail: ceo@airbrushaction.com
ISBN: 0-9637336-4-8
Printed in Singapore

Table of Contents (artists)

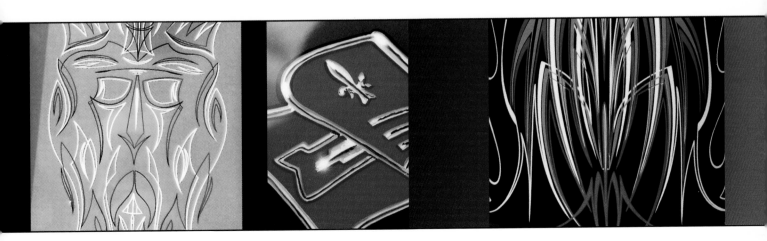

Introduction

Embellishment of non-human-powered transportation is believed to have started as early as 2600 B.C. by the Mesopotamians. It seems to be the nature of mankind to stand out from what is normal: to be original, unique, custom.

Kenneth Howard is commonly referred to as the father of modern pinstriping. More than 50 years later, his designs are still copied by stripers worldwide. Striping has also gone through many interpretations by artists who don't follow the Von Dutch school of thought. Various styles have evolved from these classic pinstripe masters who dared to be different.

The mindset of the pinstriping community has dramatically changed from closely guarding the 'secrets' of the trade and discouraging competition in any way possible to a feeling of keeping the art form alive by spreading the knowledge and educating a whole new generation of pinstriping artists. New products are hitting the market—instructional DVDs, new brush designs, and equipment—that dramatically accelerate learning. The present is bright and the future will be brighter as innovations are explored by artists worldwide in one of the fastest growing art forms ever. Now anyone with the desire can create his or her own unique expressions for all to see.

When human travel evolves into solar-powered, anti-gravitational supersonic personal transportation, you can count on it being embellished by some creative human descendant who will talk about the great masters of the old days... you and me, my brothers.

Stripe on,
—*Steve Kafka*

Brush Trimming

TOO IMPORTANT TO BE IGNORED.

All professional pinstripers trim their brushes to achieve maximum performance. Without trimming the straggler hairs from the tip—and sometimes hair from the belly—of a brush, you'll experience unwanted "scratch lines" and the inability to achieve a fine point, among other things. Chris Mack, of Mack Brush Company, agrees, but cautions that "cutting too much off the tip, a common mistake, will butcher the brush. And, although most every pro striper has his or her way of trimming a brush, the concept behind trimming the tip is basically the same."

I generally trim two parts of the brush: the tip and/or the belly, depending upon the performance I'm after.

TRIMMING TO ACHIEVE TIGHT CORNERS.

I trim the belly hairs to make the brush more user friendly in executing tight turns. Otherwise, a full belly of hair can get in the way. However, you'll need all the belly hair for pulling long straight lines.

UNIVERSAL TRIMMING

Before using a brand new brush, I strongly recommend that you remove the overextending or straggling hairs at the tip. Beginners tend to cut off too much, which ruins the brush. Over-cutting renders a blunt, and unwanted, tip. A sharp, pointed tip is what you're after.

Often, new brushes come somewhat starched from the manufacturer. Mack Brush Company, for example, uses sugar water to preserve a brush's hair during shipping. This treatment must be removed with paint thinner or mineral spirits before use. After dipping the brush into thinner, use a rag to further remove chemicals and excess moisture. Next, re-dip the brush into thinner or brush oil, shape your brush hairs to a tip, and then trim those pesky protruding straggler hairs.

> **TIP:** "...THE MORE HAIR YOU EXTRACT, THE SHORTER YOUR PULLED LINE WILL BE BECAUSE THE BELLY HAIR SERVES AS THE BRUSH'S "FUEL TANK" OR PAINT RESERVOIR."

STEP1: Here, I point to the paddle of the handle located above the blue wrap or thread.

STEP 2: I turn the brush over to use the paddle as a sort of cutting block for my hair removal surgery.

STEP 3: Typically, I trim between one-fifth and one-eighth of the brush's belly hairs.

Step 4: The hair is cut away.

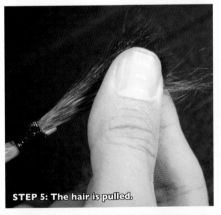

STEP 5: The hair is pulled.

STEP 6: The excess revealed.

STEP 7: Dip the brush to remove the starch and to accurately trim the tip.

Removing overextending or straggling hairs. A sharp pointed tip is what you're after.

ANDY Anderson

SUPPLIES:

Paint Media: House of Kolor® Striping Urethanes
Brushes: Hanover #00 Brushes
Other: House of Kolor® Striping Reducer (U-00),
Saral paper, Stabilo pencil, lacquer thinner
one-inch masking tape, mineral spirits

Andy Anderson is a true renaissance man of art, capable of doing anything from fine art to custom painting to pinstriping, and more—and he's world-class at all of them!

Anderson and his wife Sherry (also an artist) have been running Anderson Studio in Nashville since its humble beginnings in the early 1970s when Andy was painting vans and motorcycles. Business grew to the point that he was able to hire a second artist in 1976.

"That was during the big van craze of murals, and a lot of designs," Anderson says. They kept at it, painting two to five vans a week, and in 1978, one of his custom jobs appeared on the cover of *Time* magazine. "That's big stuff for a guy who's 17 years old," he says.

Andy also made a name for himself in the world of album covers, a natural for an artist from Nashville. His creativity helped him find unconventional ways to create art for the music industry. For example, he adapted Jimmy Buffet's album art, and airbrushed it as a huge mural for Buffet's tour bus.

Digital media and computer tools may have taken over the world of commercial art, but Andy keeps an old-school approach. "I installed a number of computers for the folks doing production at my screenprinting business,"

he says. "But all my renderings and design work are by hand. I use pencils, markers, you know, traditional tools."

Still, his painting career is a technical journey of sorts. From early airbrush murals and detail work, Andy has moved on to the full technology of prepping, priming, base-coating, and clear-coating. . . all dependent on evolving chemistry and techniques.

Andy prefers to save time by employing his friend and master striper, Rick Harris. However, when Anderson does his own pinstripe work, he uses a unique approach that involves a lot of preparation in the design.

Step 1

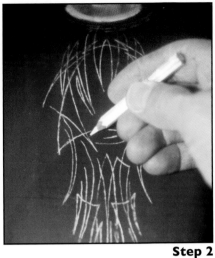

Step 2

Step 3

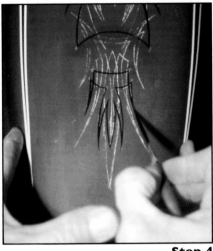

Step 4

Step 5

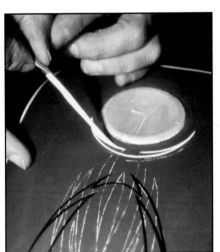

Step 6

Step 1:
First, I sketched my striping layout on tracing paper. I'm not comfortable with free-forming a design, so I always plan ahead. Designing on paper allows me to do half a design, fold it over, and retrace it on the other side. It also gives me a good centerline for positioning. I use Saral paper as if it were carbon paper to transfer my art to the tank. A pounce pattern and chalk does the same thing.

Step 2:
I touched up any missed areas with a Stabilo pencil. The existing residue was wiped away with water later.

Step 3:
I set up the paint and paletted the brush until it was properly loaded and ready to stripe. I usually use enamel-coated scrap from a paper company as a palette; a phone book also works well.

Step 4:
I began the design with House of Kolor black. I continued to load paint and palette the brush as I worked, trying to maintain a thin line.

Step 5:
Switching to white with a clean brush and using fresh reducer, I paletted the brush.

Step 6:
To make the curves around the gas filler, I rotated the brush between my fingers. This takes practice. Through the rest of the design, I tried to maintain a proper and consistent line thickness, paying careful attention to symmetry and weight.

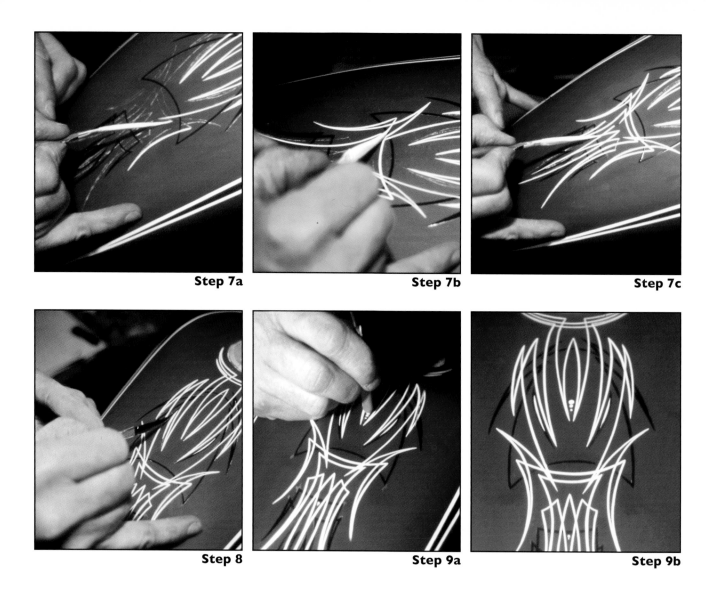

Step 7a

Step 7b

Step 7c

Step 8

Step 9a

Step 9b

Step 7a, b & c:
I worked the white over the black, using both hands for steady lines.

Step 8:
I returned to black and added a stripe around the two white dagger strokes.

Step 9a & b:
For a nice old-school touch, I loaded the pointed end of the brush handle with white and added a few dot pattern accents.

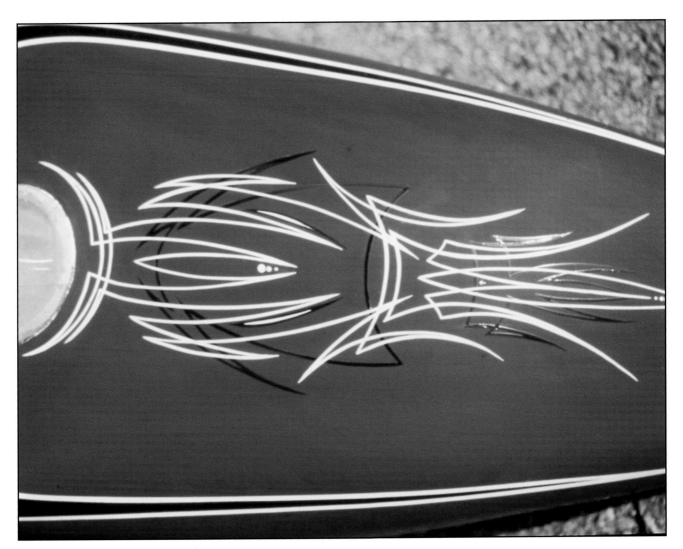

The Finished Piece:
Notice how the pinstriped design further complements the scallops, giving the project that old-school look.

GARY Berg

SUPPLIES:

Paint Media: 1-Shot® lettering enamels
Brushes: Xcaliber #0 striping brushes
Other: Rapid-Prep wax and grease remover, masking tape, Stabilo pencil, magnetic guide, Xcaliber Art-Kups, 3M™ fine line masking tape (#215), aluminum ruler

In the mid-1960s, Gary Berg pored over the pages of *Hot Rod* and *Car Craft* magazines. He was especially interested in the wild creations of George Barris and Ed Roth. Working hard at various odd-jobs helped him save enough money to buy a Honda 90cc motorcycle at the tender age of 13. Since he didn't have enough money for a car (and couldn't have driven one legally anyway), he decided to paint his motorcycle in a manner that mimicked the schemes gracing the car magazines he loved. His father had an airbrush, an air compressor, a basic knowledge of auto painting, and a lot of patience, so he helped Berg with the project. After seeing Berg's work, a friend asked him to paint a dirt bike. Using Mack brushes and Dulux enamel, he was soon applying the shaky lines of a novice pinstriper to his friends' motorcycles and their older brothers' cars.

Back in high school, Berg began working summers and on weekends in the custom paint and pinstriping shop of Mike Clines. It was there that Berg learned of 1-Shot® and Grumbacher 1010 striping brushes. After two years with Clines, Berg attended college and pinstriped part-time. By graduation, Berg's lines had become as straight as a laser beam and his work was gracing the pages of the magazines he loved. So he put his geology degree to immediate use by going to work full time as a painter/pinstriper for a local body shop, California Customs.

At 25, Berg and a friend opened their own body and paint shop. It was during this time he met Dale Weber and began to emulate his lettering style. Berg sold his business two years later and began to focus on mobile pinstriping and lettering while occasionally picking up a spray gun and painting complete custom jobs.

For the next 20 years his work primarily consisted of pinstriping for dealerships and body shops, where he had to learn to be as fast as the wind in order to make

money. Between 1991 and 1994, he established himself as one of the world's fastest pinstripers while competing at Letterhead events. He also became one of the only two 1-Shot®-sponsored Pinstripe Racing Team members, representing the manufacturer at the Lead East Car Show in Parsippany, New Jersey. There he met Alan Johnson, who came up with Berg's moniker, "Left Coaster," the name of his business today.

Among Berg's more notable projects are the world's largest motorcycle on display at the Guinness Book of Records Museum in Hollywood, the SSC Thrust Race car that broke the speed of sound, a flamed 1950 Ford at Disneyland's California Adventure in Anaheim, and more than 2,500 limousines for O'Gara Coachworks and Kelly Stageways.

Step 1

Step 2

Step 3

Step 4

Step 5

Step 6

Step 1:
I started with bare aluminum cut to 21-by-21-inches. I cleaned the aluminum of all impurities—oil, oxides, salts and fingerprints—with a solution of pure acetic acid.

Step 2:
I grinded the prepped metal with a coarse grit of about 36-40 for a deeper cut. The deeper the grooves, the higher angle of attack for the light to reflect, which enhances the "dancing lights" effect.

Step 3:
The preliminary grinding was done with a large-diameter grinder to make a fairly large, uniform backdrop texture.

Step 4:
Using a small die grinder, I added small flourishes. The swirl patterns were dictated by differing speeds of movement across the surface, and by different angles. Experiment to discover what works best for you.

Step 5:
After grinding the panel to my satisfaction, I blew off the surface residue using a powerful, well-filtered air blower. You don't want any oil from the compressor on the panel, and don't touch it until it's cleared. Contaminants, including fingerprints, may not show up at first but in time will corrode or oxidize the surface under the paint. A good amount of clear was applied to fill in all grinder grooves and create a smooth finish for the artwork. Some color sanding and additional clearing is advised.

Step 6:
After the clear completely dried, I applied a cut vinyl paint mask (of my business name) to the finished panel. This will be used for the faded background transition.

Step 7

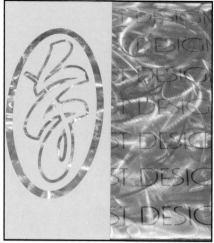
Step 8

Step 9

Step 10

Step 11

Step 12

Step 7:

I started with the bottom of the panel and sprayed a couple of coats of kandy tangerine. I masked off the rest of the copy so that only the lowest line of text was exposed. Then I moved the masking paper up one level of text and sprayed the lower line and the one immediately above it. This process was repeated all the way to the top of the panel. The subsequent spraying of a new layer with the previous ones created the transition from light to dark—good old-fashioned "tape fading" with some text thrown in.

Step 8:

After removing the mask, I applied a thin layer of clear to protect the surface for subsequent steps and handling. I applied the outermost parts of the logo for the beveling process. Remember to start from the background and work toward the front; this saves a lot of time in masking and re-masking.

Step 9:

I painted the outer bevel using a mixture of clear, black or white, and pearl. Here Murano pearl, with its brilliant quality and finer grain, was employed. I added about 5 percent black or white to the clear. Light and dark achieves the high and low quality you're after. Once the bevel was painted, I removed the mask and colored all but the inside of the oval, which was painted using Metal Flake Kandy tangerine/kandy fire red in a 50/50 mix.

Step 10:

With the oval completely covered, a drop shadow using straight black, was airbrushed to give the oval a floating effect.

Step 11:

My favorite concoction, Slime Lime, was used to paint the background. This anti-freeze/toxic-green color was made by mixing lemon yellow and highly pigmented green toner with clear. Colleagues don't call me "Slimer" for nothing.

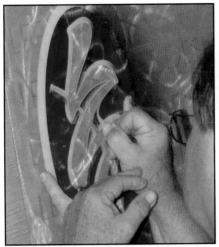

Step 13a

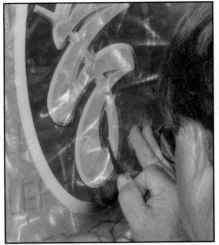

Step 13b

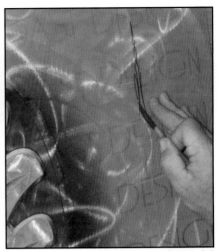

Step 14

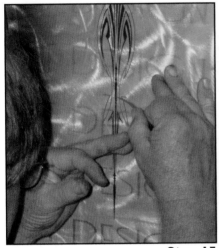

Step 15

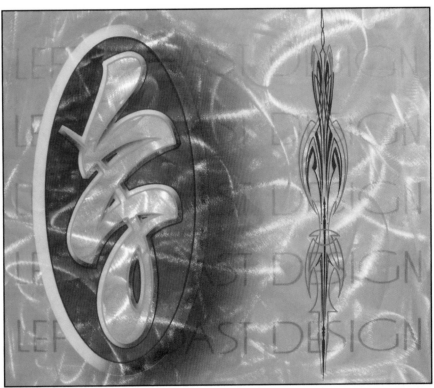

The Finished Piece

Step 12:
After removing the mask, I cleared the entire panel with top coat clear in preparation for pinstriping, outlining and design.

Step 13:
I outlined the logo with a Mack 00. I used lime green for the inner edge of the bevel, and purple for the outer edge.

Step 14:
I started pinstriping with a Dominican Sword striping brush and 1-Shot® lead paint that was manufactured in the 1970s. For continuity, I used the same purple.

Step 15:
I selected tangerine/fire red to complete the design and bring the piece together.

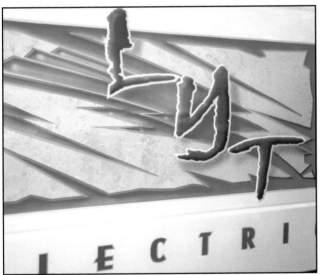

JIM Bradley

SUPPLIES:

Paint Media: PPG base coats and House Of Kolor® paints
Brushes: Mack 20 striping brush, Langnickel 749, Grumbacher graining and fan brushes
Other: Gold size, patent gold leaf

In the summer of 1954, when Jim Bradley was 16, his father took him to El Mirage Dry Lake for a day of racing. It was there that a set of hashed lines on the grille shell of a 1932 Ford caught his eye and curiosity. Upon closer examination, Bradley noticed a pinstriped design, and from then on he was hooked. More than 50 years later, his love affair with the art form still surges.

To the chagrin of his parents, he would practice his craft on metal kitchen cabinets, cups, glassware, and just about any suitable household item he could find. Bradley was soon good enough to impress his friends and pinstripe their older brothers' hot rods. His first paying job was a 1954 Chrysler Imperial.

He eventually started pinstriping out of the back of Eddie's Speed Shop in Bakersfield, California, and before long had his own place. After accompanying Gary Quinn, of Quinn Equipment, to Southern California to have Quinn's 1933 Ford Coupe pinstriped, Bradley was invited by famed pinstriper Von Dutch to share the job. The car was chrome yellow, so they agreed to stripe the belt line in red. Bradley started at the left front while Dutch started on the right. As they rounded the quarter-panels and met in the back, Bradley was flabbergasted to see that Dutch, true to his eccentric reputation, had switched to green. The car exists to this day, unchanged, green on one side and red on the other.

In Fresno, Bradley and local giant Shaky Jake created the "Fresno Line" when they tried, and failed, to emulate the well-known San Francisco striper Tommy the Greek's signature stripe. In trying to hide the inadequacies of that attempt, they created a design that remains popular today.

Bradley later served in Vietnam for four years as a Navy S.E.A.L. and eventually joined the C.I.A. While stationed at Point Mugu Naval Air Station in Oxnard, California, he practically invented the term "multi-

tasking," working as art director at Point Mugu, operating his own custom van fabrication shop, teaching art at Ventura College at night, and serving on weekends as art director for *Vans and Trucks* magazine. *Vans and Trucks* also produced *Chevy Power*, *Ford Power* and *Street Vans*, and it was there that Jim prototyped a new magazine called *Lowrider*.

Bradley continues his trade in a one-man shop in Yuba City, California, and has no plans to retire. His mantra: "The master in the art of living makes little distinction between his work and his play, his labor and his leisure, his mind and his body, his education and his recreation, his love and his religion. He hardly knows which is which. He simply pursues his vision of excellence in whatever he does, leaving others to decide whether he is working or playing. To him, he is always doing both."

Step 1

Step 2

Step 3

Step 4

Step 5

Step 6

Step 1:
Before priming, the 1932 Ford dash was degreased, sanded, had its imperfections filled in, and then re-sanded.

Step 2:
I filled in all sanding scratches and pinholes with filler putty.

Step 3:
After the primer fully cured, I wet-sanded in preparation for the color coat.

Step 4:
The color coat is a single-stage tan—a mix of yellow, blue, white, black, and orange toners—applied with a DeVilbiss touch-up gun. Single-stage paint does not require a clear coat.

Step 5:
I started the wood grain with a fan brush, mixing root beer, yellow, and tangerine kandy toners in different strengths, with clear used as a glaze.

Step 6:
This close-up shows how the brush was jogged, swiveled, and pulled at different speeds to give the random grain effect. Loading the brush heavier on one side is also a way to build color depth and grain strength.

Step 7

Step 8

Step 9

Step 10

Step 11

Step 12

Step 7:
I made subsequent passes with the brush, loaded in intervals of varying amounts, to build the grain texture. Be sure to run the grain in the same direction.

Step 8:
Not wanting to destroy my old grainer-flagger (a rare antique brush made of horsehair) in the urethanes, I used a cheap brush of ox hair. I "combed" the brush by running a single-edged razor blade just slightly off the direction of the hair to thin and stagger the length of the bristles.

Step 9:
The homemade flagger was paletted using the toners and clear.

Step 10:
I finished up the grain with the flagger. This is for the fine grain that is inconsistent throughout the whole piece, like the stippling effect of oak.

Step 11:
After the grain completely dried, I applied full wet coats of kandy root beer and then clear. Root beer can be made with a mix of orange, red, yellow and black toners.

Step 12:
Before the size was applied, I used a pounce bag of Kaolin finely powdered clay (the stuff that Milk of Magnesia is made from). It prevents the leaf from adhering to any surfaces that have not been sized. Here, I used a plastic tape to create a hard edge on one side. This makes it easier to "mop" on a wide stripe of the almost invisible size by just concentrating on one edge. Masking tape allows the size to bleed through, causing a jagged edge. I use 24-hour size for this purpose because it can withstand urethane clear much better and with much less incidence of wrinkling.

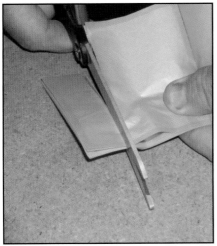

Step 13

Step 14

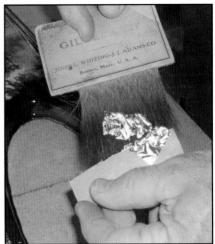

Step 15

Step 16

Step 17

Step 18

Step 13:
If you don't have a roll of patent leaf handy, just cut the book of loose leaf into roughly 3/4-inch strips. The leaf is better conserved when cut into strips.

Step 14:
I "charged" the gilding brush by fanning it in my hair. This slight charge of static electricity and just enough oil from the hair helps attract and hold a piece of gold leaf. Another method is to put a very small amount of petroleum jelly on your finger, rub it together with your thumb, and then palette the brush between your thumb and forefinger to impart just enough oil to pick up the leaf.

Step 15:
The charged gilding brush "acquired" the leaf, which was then placed on the size.

Step 16:
After the leaf was applied, I matted it down with my finger for good coverage and adhesion. This is necessary to avoid any pinholes and "holidays" in the leaf. Voids may be filled using more leaf, as it sticks only to the size.

Step 17:
I burnished the leaf with genuine surgical quality "Bakersfield cotton." This gives the leaf a high polish and removes any extra particles of leaf not held by the size.

Step 18:
This 3/8-inch stripe needed an "engine-turning" tool of approximately the same or slightly larger diameter, such as an old 38-40 Krag cartridge with a .410 shotgun felt overshot wad glued to the base and wrapped with velveteen.

Step 19

Step 20

Step 19:
The leaf was engine-turned by spinning the tool approximately one-half turn and then overlapping the turns by one-half the diameter. This produced a finish that really made the leaf shimmer and dance in reflected light.

Step 20:
After the piece was cleared, I applied a bordering stripe to cover any small fragmentation of the edges and to give a finished look to the stripe.

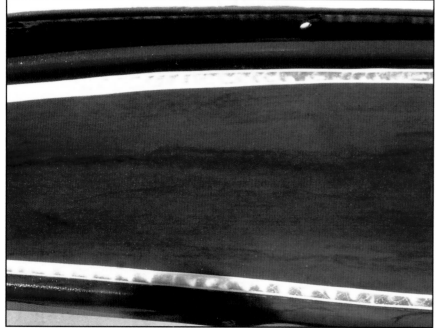

The Finished Piece:
This close-up shows the grain and engine-turned leaf.

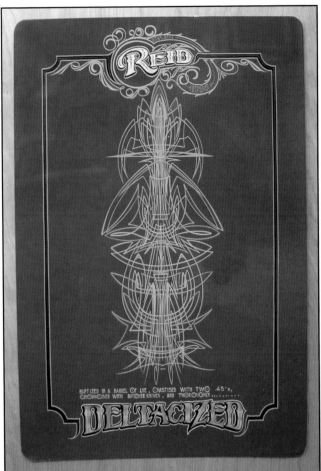

27

JOE Broxterman

SUPPLIES:

Paint Media: I-Shot® Lettering Enamels
Brushes: Mack, Dauber's Equalizer and LazerLines
Other: Ditzler enamel reducer. X-Acto knives, Stabilo pencils, Catalyst, PPG-DX 393 wax and grease remover, Soft Scrub, and buffing compound

Working on the road...

I use the tailgate of my pickup truck as a bench. I've pop-riveted a piece of .050 aluminum to the inside of the tailgate to make it flat and easier to clean. My tools of the trade include a cardboard palette box, paint in plastic bottles, Scott Rags, a brush kit, an empty gallon can for scrap reducer, window cleaner, and assorted garbage.

The palette box is made from an old quarter-panel box from a body shop. The cutouts hold, left to right: reducer with catalyst, two cups of color, and a cup to clean brushes. Closing the lid keeps dirt out and prevents the paint on the palette from drying too quickly on hot days. Next is my box of colors, all in plastic bottles kept upside down. The dividers are made from thin aluminum. I've also got a spot to store some receipt books and a couple of pens.

designs and outlining flames, I use Mack Brushes. For long straight lines I use either Dauber's Equalizer or LazerLines brushes.

The Project:

A custom bike painter delivered this project—bike parts that had been painted, cleared, and wet-sanded with 1000-grit sandpaper—with simple, clear instructions: "The customer said do whatever moves you...Go nuts!"

My brush box contains striping, lettering, and Lavallee pictorial brushes, X-acto knives, Stabilo pencils, paper cups, quarter-inch tape, brush oil, LazerLines logo screens, and business cards. The plastic bottles contain catalyst, anti-static (PPG-DX 393), enamel reducer, wax and grease remover, Soft Scrub, and buffing compound. For striping

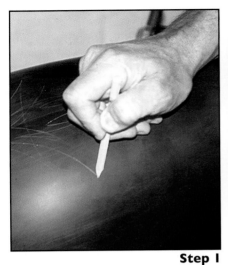

Step 1

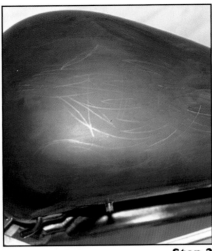

Step 2

Step 3

Step 4

Step 5

Step 6

Step 1:
I lightly laid out the design on the sanded parts with a Stabilo pencil. This served simply as an idea of the stripe design and was subject to change.

Step 2:
I finished the sketch of the design on the tank, and...

Step 3:
... the fender is finished.

Step 4:
After premixing the first of three shades of purple (the striping was cleared later), I added a 50/50 mix of 1-Shot® catalyst and Ditzler DT-870 reducer.

Step 5:
My paint cart for shop work contains brushes, airbrushes, rulers, etc. The palette on top of the cart is a cheap clipboard screwed on to hold an old magazine or anything with glossy pages. Childproof caps from reducer cans are the perfect size to mix small amounts of catalyst.
Tip: Once catalyst is added to reducer or paint, it's only good for a few hours, so mix only what you think you'll use.

Step 6:
I loaded the brush with paint by working it back and forth on the palette.

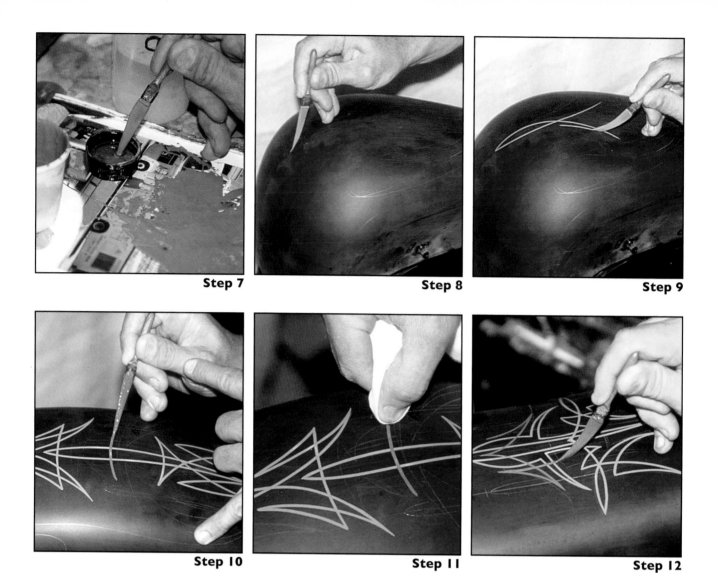

Step 7

Step 8

Step 9

Step 10

Step 11

Step 12

Step 7:
I dipped the tip of the brush in the reducer/catalyst mix about a quarter-inch, then re-paletted. If you over-reduce, the brush won't track well, and too much paint will flow to the tip of the brush and drip. This is something you have to practice and develop a feel for.

Step 8:
Being right-handed, I started on the left side of the tank. There are two reasons righties work left to right: There's less chance of putting your fingers in the paint, and it's often easier to achieve symmetry by matching the right side to the left. I started with the teardrop in the middle.

Step 9:
Develop your design by working left to right and top to bottom, flipping the tank to duplicate your design on the opposite side.
Tip: Do the first color on all pieces before moving on to the second; by the time the last piece is finished, the first piece is dry and ready for its second color.

Step 10:
I switch to a darker purple, my second color. Start at the top of the design, left to right.

Step 11:
Mistakes can be fixed by doubling up a soft paper shop towel or cloth. With a little wax and grease remover on the rag, push your mistake back into the line. The wax and grease remover is important to prevent a "ghost" from appearing after the clearcoat is applied. Once the design starts to take shape, mistakes become harder to fix. If your fingers are too big for the little fixes, break out the DeWayne Connot-authorized signature model pinstripe eraser! It's actually a tool for cuticles that you can buy at a cosmetic store. The soft rubber tip on it can be used to fix mistakes. I picked up this tip from Connot, who learned it from Gary Steele.

Step 12:
I painted the second color identical to the first.

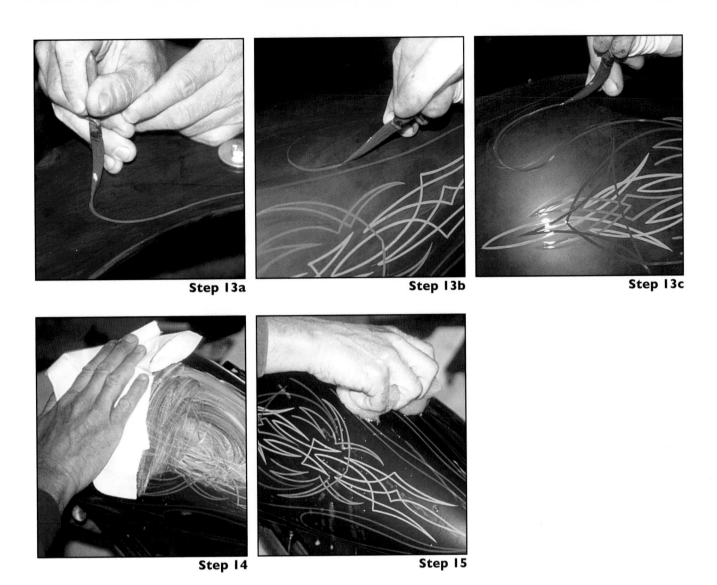

Step 13a

Step 13b

Step 13c

Step 14

Step 15

Step 13:
With the third color, the darkest purple, it was time for flames. I started at the loop, 12 o'clock on the left side. I pulled down toward the tip. On the right side, I started at 10 o'clock, striping over what I had already done to get the line thickness. Then, I moved down toward the next tip. After the final color, I let it dry overnight. The next morning, I gave it a good cleaning with Soft Scrub and water before delivering.

Step 14:
Soft Scrub has a very fine grit, which is perfect for removing leftover Stabilo lines and ghosts.

Step 15:
I rinsed off the suds with water. While the job was still wet, I looked for any remaining Stabilo lines or ghosts. If any appear, blow it dry, re-clean with Soft Scrub, and rinse again.

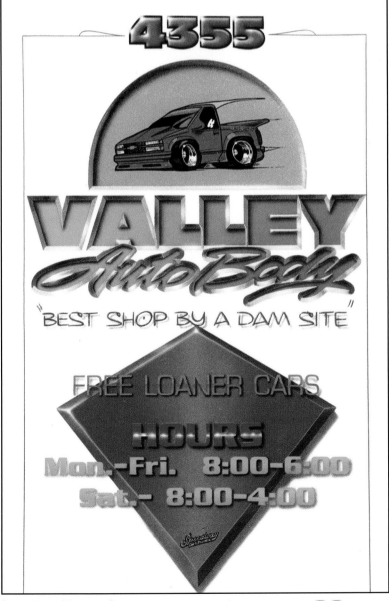

STEVE Cox

SUPPLIES:
Paint Media: 1-Shot® lettering enamels
Brushes: #000 Mack pinstriping brushes
Other: R-M 900 Pre-Kleano wax & silicone remover,
70% isopropyl alcohol, regular pure gum turpentine,
Stabilo art pencils, ¼-inch masking tape, mineral spirits

Steve Cox grew up in Pomona, California, the heartland of custom cars and rock & roll, and situated only a few blocks from the Los Angeles County Fair Grounds, home to the NHRA's Winternationals. As a teenager in the 1960s, Cox played guitar in studio sessions for United Artists records where he found himself rubbing elbows with his musical heroes and being deluged with requests from bands to employ his painting skills to letter drumheads and stage banners. Eventually he realized he was having more fun with the paintbrush than with the guitar.

During a stint as a medic with the 101st Airborne in Vietnam, Cox managed to continue his craft; helicopters and personnel carriers became his canvas. He started his pinstriping and graphics business in 1975, with the majority of his work done at car shows, rod runs and motorcycle rallies. He continues to disdain the "peel-and-stick" mentality of some younger car enthusiasts, and is dedicated to sharing the "lost art" of pinstriping with the new generation. "It's cool to watch their faces as I drag a freehand line down the side of a street rod, or do an impromptu center piece design on a motorcycle tank." He and his wife of 32 years, Lynda, have two sons and live in Abilene, Texas.

The Project:
One of my customers just finished building a new racecar for his wife. Thank God he's a purist, and won't tolerate stick-on vinyl graphics on any of his cars. The car already had a nice metallic blue finish, so he decided to have me single-stage the project. Single-staging is doing the striping and graphics right onto the vehicle without regard to sanding, clearcoating and buffing. This is exactly what 1-Shot® paint is designed to do.

As for the car's body and fenders, I laid out the graphics, taped them off, and painted them using 1-Shot® and a Mack broad-liner brush. With a little practice using the broad-liner and pure gum turpentine to palette with, you can have a finished piece that almost looks like it was sprayed.

Once the car's new graphics were complete, it was time for a finishing touch. I thought the top of the fiberglass hood air-scoop needed a little splash of true pinstriping. Since the vertical surfaces of the car have a contemporary look, I figured I could get away with a more classical approach on the horizontal plane of the hood's scoop.

Step 1

Step 2a

Step 2b

Step 3a

Step 3b

Step 4

Step 1:

There should be no shortcuts when it comes to prepping the surface to be striped. I started with a good quality grease & wax remover, wiped the surface down, and then sprayed alcohol over the area and wiped the surface again. I used a plastic spray bottle and regular rubbing alcohol (70% Isopropyl), available at any grocery store. This seemed to remove any residue that inevitably was left by the grease & wax remover and made the surface squeaky clean.

Step 2a & b:

I've seen excellent designs fail simply because the striper was just a bit off center with the centerline. I started by applying a vertical centerline with 1/4-inch masking tape, then marked light Stabilo pencil lines on both edges of the tape. I recommend not getting carried away with a guideline as that takes away from some of the freedom and spontaneity that is an important part of pinstriping.

Step 3a & b:

I started the freeform, ad-lib part of the design. For the first part, I used a new uncut Mack #000 striping brush. Trimming and cutting striping brushes is something you'll just have to experiment with. Working from one side to the other, I began building the basic frame of the design. Since I matched the paint to the graphics on the racecar, I started with process blue, one of the brighter dominant colors. I used some of the more contrasting colors later as an accent.

Step 4:

To add an opposing point of interest and break up the vertical rhythm of the design, I tossed in a horizontal line, making sure to attach the line to another point of the design frame for good measure.

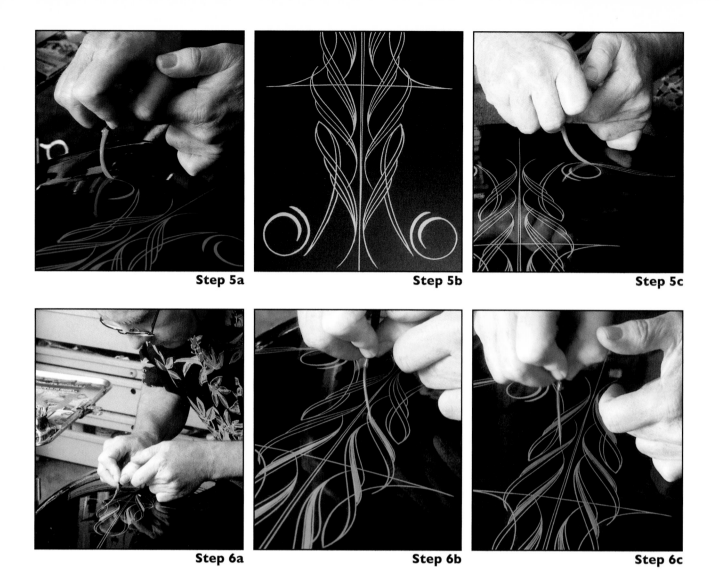

Step 5a   Step 5b   Step 5c

Step 6a   Step 6b   Step 6c

Step 5:
Using another Mack #000, trimmed down a bit, I added a couple of scrolls. I've used Macks for scroll work for many years. Many pinstripers use an outliner brush for this purpose. To scroll with a Mack brush is somewhat unnatural, so it requires much practice.

Step 6:
After adding a few more base lines, the first stage was complete. I added orange as an inlay color to the open areas of the design. Notice that I didn't fill in all of the open segments; to do so would make the design appear bulky. Next, I used magenta to lightly accent the top of each orange-inlayed section. This also serves to give the illusion of a subtle color transition.

Step 7a | **Step 7b** | **Step 7c**

Step 8a | **Step 8b** | **The Finished Piece**

Step 7a, b, c:

The illusion of one color wrapping around another color has always been a staple in my work. For this part I used the base gray that was used on the side of the car. The subtle variation in brush pressure is what makes the line appear to flow from background to foreground and back again. If your luck runs anything like mine, this is where the "Static Gremlin" will attack. Static electricity is one of the worst enemies of any pinstriper who works on fiberglass, plastic, Plexiglas® or any substrate that can build a static charge. To eliminate static, just spray some alcohol on the backside of the air scoop.

Step 8a & b:

To bring out the other colors of the graphic, I added a few colorful accents with orange and yellow. Since I had the trusty old signature brush out, I signed the piece, put the hood back on the car and called the customer... it's ready to go racing.

Helpful Tips from Steve Cox:

Our genre has entered a realm of networking and information sharing that did not exist 20 years ago. Pinstripers will always have secret recipes and shortcuts they keep close to the vest but for the most part, newcomers to the craft have a wealth of information available to them. More old-timers are willing to answer questions, and magazines and books, like the one you're reading, have helped facilitate a new, welcoming era.

Although every pinstriper has his or her own way of doing things, here are a few tips. Some of them were passed along by fellow pinstripers, and others were discovered the hard way, through trial and error.

1. 70% isopropyl alcohol is valuable in the prep process. It removes any residue the pre-clean solution leaves behind and it gives you a squeaky-clean surface.

2. Try using turpentine to palette when using 1-Shot®. This may be a little radical to some, but it'll give the paint a workable consistency and it's great for hot weather or for working outdoors. I know it stinks. Don't bathe in it, just use it sparingly to palette your brush. Use mineral spirits for clean-up to keep you and your nose on friendly terms.

3. For killer striping and lettering gold, mix Cres-Lite Metallic Powder into 1-Shot® 4006 Super Gloss Tinting Clear. The real secret is to use the super-fine grade of gold powder. Cres-Lite offers several colors in their bronzing powder line, but not all powders are super-fine.

4. For quick script lettering, you can't beat the 4901 series of synthetic outliners available from the Dick Blick Company.

5. A lot of pinstripers still use transmission fluid, motor oil, and all other sorts of greasy petroleum products to oil their brushes. I want you to know that you can still purchase a true brush oil from Wall Dog Products in Hamilton, Ohio. Wall Dog Brush Oil is a real treat for the instruments of our craft.

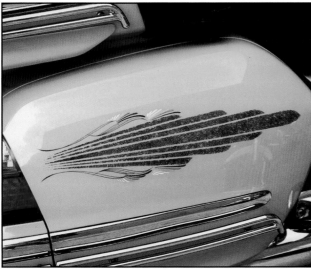
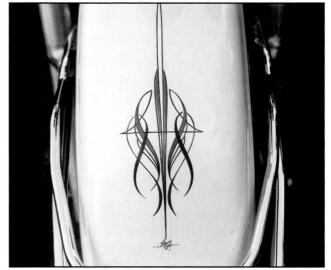

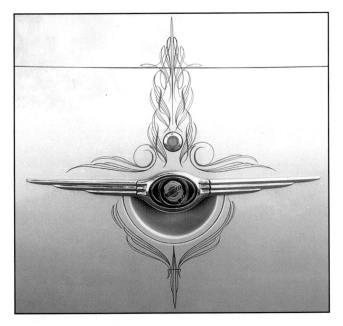

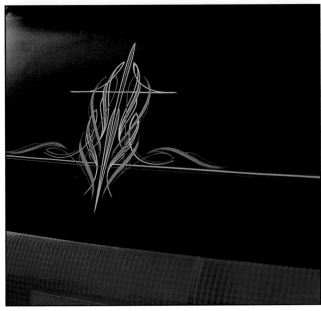

LYLE *Fisk*

SUPPLIES:
Paint Media: 1-Shot® lettering enamels and House of Kolor® striping urethanes
Brushes: Mack, Scharff, and Cosmo brands

In 1955, I started pinstriping in a small sign shop. I was car-crazy and for me striping was as magical as a David Blaine TV stunt. My boss showed me how to load and hold the brush, and then laid the brush down on the palette and said, "Develop your own style and create what you think it should look like." I striped everything in sight—the water cooler, the refrigerator, the bathtub.

I'm lucky to be able to do what I love. I can't wait to go to work every day, in my own full-blown custom shop where I help make dreams come true on cars, hot rods, boats, bikes, etc. I could write about all the neat things I've done over the past 47 years, but it would take up the rest of this book.

Look at the photo of my first sign kit below. I made it in 1956 and lettered and striped it in 1958. Over the years, I painted over the original striping and had forgotten what it used to look like. Recently, I scraped off the black paint and saved what I could of the original 1958 paintjob. It's a memento worth keeping.

Desire is the key to being a pinstriper. It should be fun. These step-by-step photos show you how I stripe, *not* how you should. All stripers have a unique style of their own, and that's the way it should be.

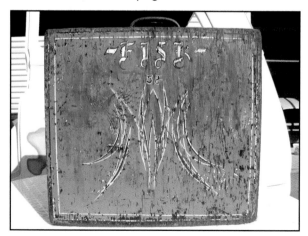

Step 1

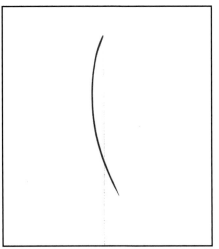

Step 2

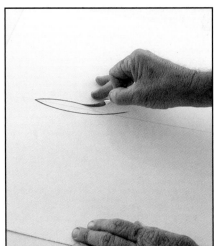

Step 3

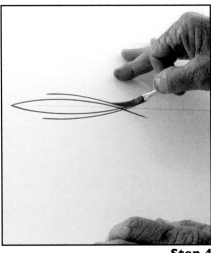

Step 4

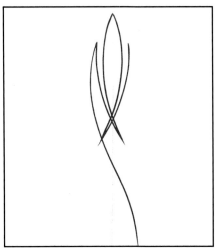

Step 5

Step 6

Step 1:
I chose a subject, cleaned the surface, and marked my center.

Step 2:
I loaded the brush with lots of 1-Shot® paint and paletted it into the brush. The most forgiving brush is a black-handled Mack 00 or 0. I started my design with the first stroke.

Step 3:
I mirrored my pattern by adding the same line on the opposite side.

Step 4:
The design developed as I continued to add lines.

Step 5:
I continued adding lines from side to side.

Step 6:
You'll begin to develop a style as you progress.

Step 7

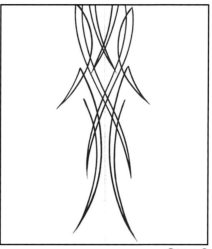

Step 8

Step 9

Step 10

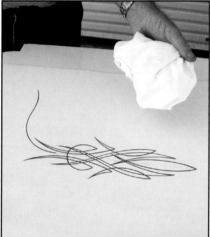

Step 11

Step 12

Step 7:
I used the center line as a guide to keep the design consistent on both sides.

Step 8:
I continued to mirror strokes as I added to the design.

Step 9:
Notice that the brush is held between the thumb and forefinger so it can roll as the stroke is pulled.

Step 10:
Pulling a nice even stroke on a semicircle came with years of experience and hours of practice.

Step 11:
Never leave a bad stripe; don't be afraid to wipe off errors. Next, I added a final stroke to the design to be repeated on the other side.

Step 12:
I filled in the additions to both sides of the design.

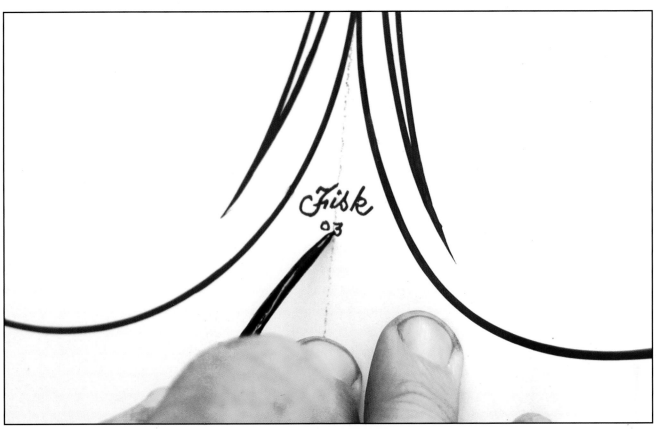

A signature for the big finish.

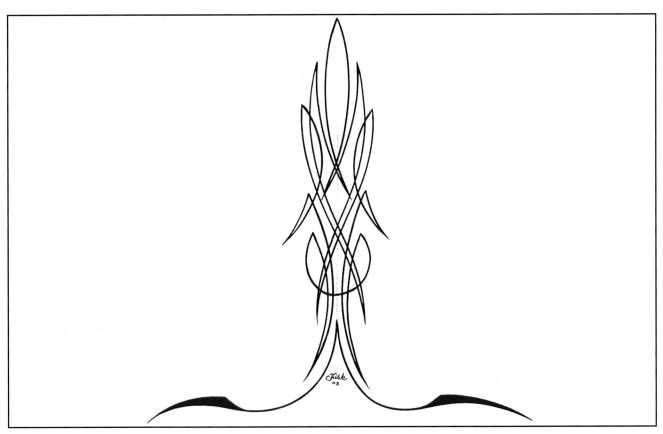

The Finished Piece

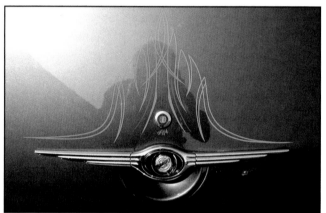

ALTON Gillespie

SUPPLIES:

Paint Media: 1-Shot® lettering enamels
Brushes: LazerLines lettering and striping brushes and a Kafka striping brush
Other: Urethane foam (SignFoam), 1/4-inch and 1/2- inch PVC sheets, Standox primer, acrylic urethane, and clearcoat

My start in pinstriping began around 1971 as an unintentional byproduct of painting signs and pictures. Starting out part-time, I found myself thrust onto the racecar scene full-time, and almost made the track my home. While shagging odd jobs in the pits, I stretched my eyeballs on all the hysterical work I saw on the funny cars coming in, and this became my school.

Early on I realized there was more to it than slopping a sign on the side. I did it all: airbrushing, using multi-colored candies, and pinstriping. When you get down to it, all are equally important, and they all work together.

Undeniably my biggest influence was Ed "Big Daddy" Roth and his crew. My junior high school teachers were always busting me for "wasting my time" in the back of the classroom copying the tiny pictures in Ed's shirt ads in car magazines. To this day I owe my eye for detail to him. These days I do a fair amount of spraying and brushing along with my wife, Canadian artist Ranger Mary. Together we operate Still on the Planet Sudios in Dallas, Texas.

The Project:

I chose to feature this Tiki head clock for its combination of brushing and spraying along with the carving I perform these days. The interplay of shape and color adds to the complexity. This project was designed for a customer's South Seas-themed party room.

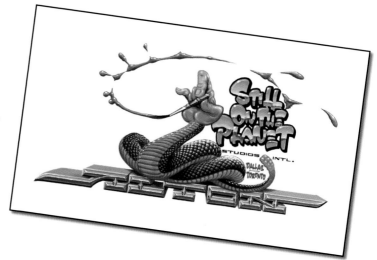

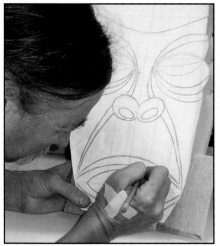

Step 1

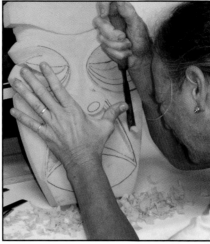

Step 2

Step 3

Step 4

Step 5

Step 6

Step 1:
My intent with this project was to blur the line between
2-D and 3-D. Here, I transferred the pattern to hard foam
using Saral transfer paper.

Step 2:
After fattening the lines with a Sharpie marker, it was time
to dig in with various wood chisels.

Step 3:
After carving, I applied plenty of primer-surfacer. Then I
sanded carefully to smooth any imperfections.

Step 4:
After sanding, I sprayed the Tiki with some automotive
colors we had laying around. I'm never afraid to base my
color choices on availability. The Honda green I used here
is almost a kandy without the aggravation, and the pink
pearl for the hat is from a Daryl Starbird car we fixed.

Step 5:
I worked off the pent-up frustration from carving by
starting off dark (reflex blue) with my stripes. I built over
that with lighter colors. Using a tape centerline makes it
easier to keep both sides even.

Step 6:
I painted the eyebrows by brushing up from the 1/4-inch
tape. This makes a clean straight edge on the bottom. I
also roughed in the basic design on the hat; later I'll outline
and stripe over it.

Step 7

Step 8

Step 9

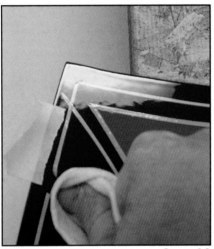

Step 10

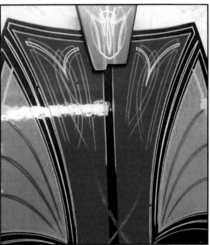

Step 11

Step 12

Step 7:
After finishing up under the nose, I painted the cheeks with polar white, and then I outlined with two shades of orange.

Step 8:
I airbrushed the end pieces with a 1955 Chevy blue and striped just enough to make them look busy. Tape was used just for spacing. Whatever makes the job easier, stand on it.

Step 9:
I cut the backboard from 1/2-inch plywood, and primed and painted it. I pulled all the long lines using a LazerLines striper. The Tiki's lower body was sawed from 1/2-inch PVC, primed, and sprayed using Honda green with Kandy shading. The hands were made of an extra layer of PVC, which I taped on to see where the stripes would go.

Step 10:
When I need a gap in the line I simply wipe through it.

Step 11:
After affixing the end pieces, I finished striping the backboard using tape only as a guide.

Step 12:
Again using tape to space with, I transferred a pattern made with the old "cattle prod" (Electro-Pounce) over the purple areas with baby powder. A lighter purple was chosen for this section. To duplicate the image on the other side, all you have to do is flip the pattern over, wipe off the powder, and pounce again.

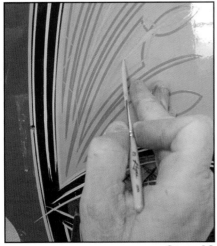

Step 13

Step 14

Step 15

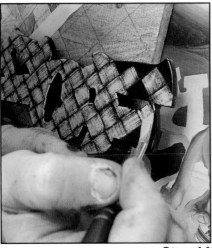

Step 16

Step 17

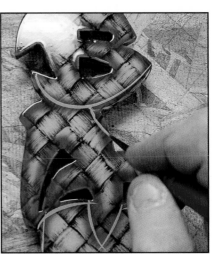

Step 18

Step 13:
Final striping involved Kafka-style flourishes using the Kafka brush. If you're going to copy the guy's stuff you'll need his brush.

Step 14:
I spared showing you how I carved the drum. Same as the head: primed, painted, and cleared. I threw in the name to fill space, then worked from there to stripe it. I forgot to shoot the final stages of it, but it's all straightforward darks building to light colors.

Step 15:
"Tiki Tom's" letters were sawed from 1/4-inch PVC, primed, airbrushed (fading yellow, orange and red), and then cleared and outlined later with black and white.

Step 16:
The "House of Bambu" letters needed a thatch effect. I started by drawing a grid with a graphite Stabilo pencil, then I dry-brushed between the lines, being careful to alternate each little square. The letters, by the way, were first cut from 1/4-inch PVC, then blacked out.

Step 17:
Using my trusty-old "I-Whut-Uh" (my nickname for my old beat-up Iwata) airbrush, I shaded the edges with kandy brown.

Step 18:
After clearing the "House of Bambu" letters, I lined them with "Rat Fink" green.

The Finished Piece:
After screwing everything together from the backside, I finished the striping and installed the clock in the mouth using hands cut from a CD (*Greatest Hits of the Monkees*), then kandy coated the hands blue and green. The clock makes it a useful appliance, and therefore gives it purpose!

Tips for Beginners
By Alton Gillespie

1. Do not be seduced by the computer. Learn from what has been designed with a brush and understand the difference. The "brushier" your work appears, the more of a premium it will command.

2. I have found that I learned a lot of what I need to know about each job while doing it. Get a good start on it and design as you go.

3. Adhesion is as important as looks on automotive finishes. A high-gloss surface is difficult for sign enamel to hang onto, so after cleaning with wax and grease remover, give it a careful wash with Ajax and water. This makes almost invisible micro-scratches that help the enamel grip the surface. For the same reason, add a little hardener to your sign colors.

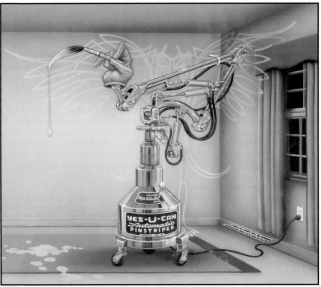

CARY *Greenwood*

SUPPLIES:
Paint Media: I-Shot® lettering enamels
Brushes: Mack 00 striping brushes
Other: Foam board for the panel

Cary Greenwood was born in Oakland, California on the day Pearl Harbor was attacked, a clue for his mother that he wasn't going to be a standard-issue kid. He took up drawing in grammar school, and while working his high-school job at a local drugstore, he would delve into the magazine rack looking for issues of *Rod and Custom*, *Car Craft*, *Hot Rod* and *Speed Age*, to read about legends like Von Dutch, Dean Jefferies, Larry Watson, and a pinstriper from Oakland named Tommy the Greek. While hanging around the neighborhood auto shop and drive-in, Greenwood soaked in the artistry of the racecars and trucks, many of them adorned with the Greek's work.

As a high school sophomore, Greenwood painted his first car lime green and headed to the Greek's nearby shop to have it striped — tear drops, of course, dark green with white trim. He was blown away by how easy Tom made striping look, and resolved to become a striper himself.

After seeing Greenwood experiment with striping on a school binder with a pen, a friend told him where to find paint supplies. In no time, friends were allowing Greenwood to practice on their cars. One day a stranger asked him how much he'd charge to stripe a car, and Greenwood was on his way to becoming a professional. He would beg his way into Roadster shows (gaining access through his friend, the late Mel Fernandes), and would seek customers car to car. Ed Roth even secured his help pinstriping fiberglass Nazi helmets.

In 1960, Greenwood, then working in a West Oakland factory, lost three fingers and the top of his little finger in a punch-press accident. He was in and out of the hospital for three years and believed his pinstriping days were over, until his phone rang one day and a man named Benny Bosberg asked if Greenwood would stripe his

model pickup. Greenwood didn't think he'd be able to, but decided to give it a shot anyway. He did it, perfectly, and Bosberg pitched him to eight or nine other customers, allowing Greenwood to regain his confidence and go on to a storied 45-year career.

In 1994 he earned the Von Dutch Award the first time it was given out at the Oakland Roadster Show. Early in 2005, he received the Tommy the Greek Award at Rick Perry's Oakland Rod Custom & Motorcycle show, making Greenwood the first striper ever to garner both awards.

Looking back, Greenwood thanks his wife, Kimberly, their children, and countless others like Tom Otis, who have helped him along the way. But it is Tommy the Greek who remains his hero, and he considers striping teardrops on his mentor's casket his greatest honor.

Step 1

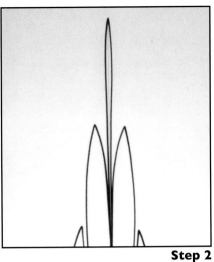

Step 2

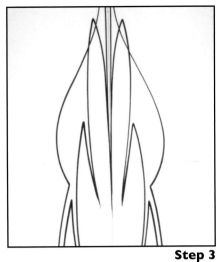

Step 3

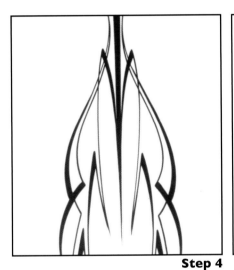

Step 4

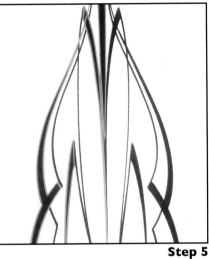

Step 5

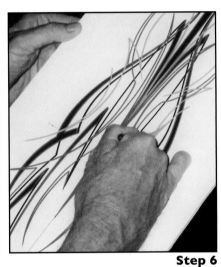

Step 6

Step 1:
With a pencil, I lightly laid out the center line top to bottom, then centered it side to side.

Step 2:
My designs always begin with a teardrop—a sign of respect for my inspiration and mentor, the late, great California striper Tommy the Greek.

Step 3:
I began building the design. I always do the left stroke first, then the right.

Step 4:
I added more of the first color, thickening some of the strokes for definition.

Step 5:
The second color was introduced freehand.

Step 6:
After finishing the second color, you can see the design filling out. Stripe freely; let the piece steer you.

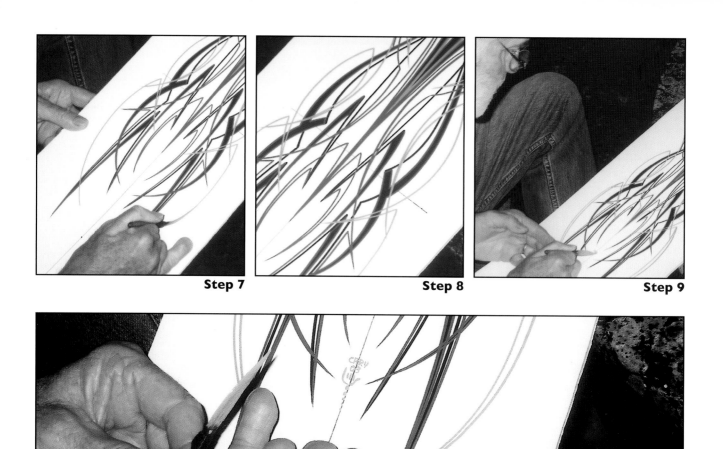

Step 7

Step 8

Step 9

Step 10

Step 7:
The third color was added by cutting across the other colors in different directions.

Step 8:
I filled out the bottom of the design with the third color.

Step 9:
After finishing the third color, I added a signature.

Step 10:
I always finish with my hand, well most of it anyway. A nice match, don't you think?

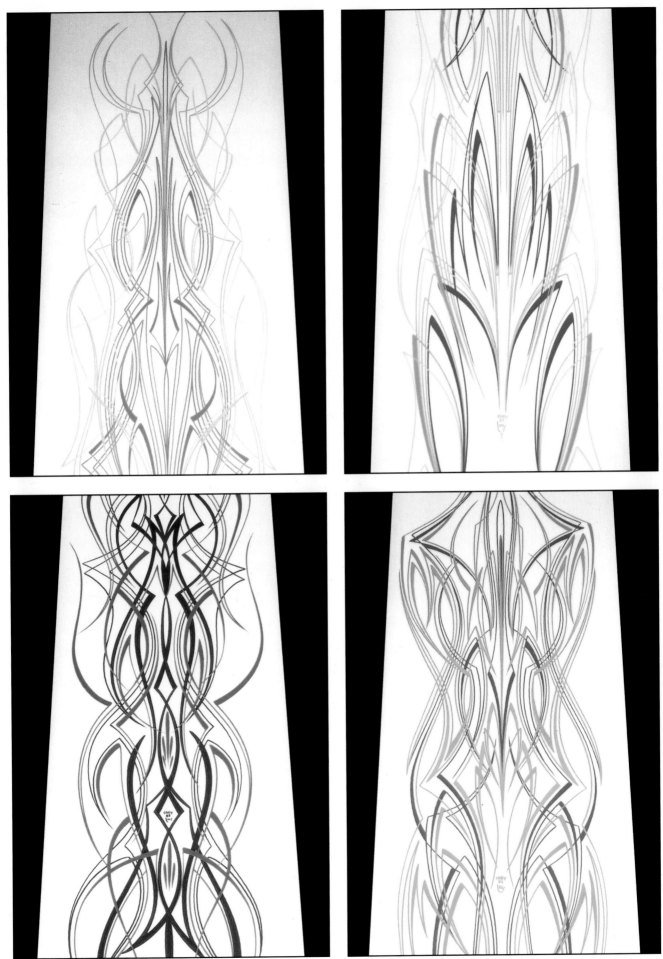

57

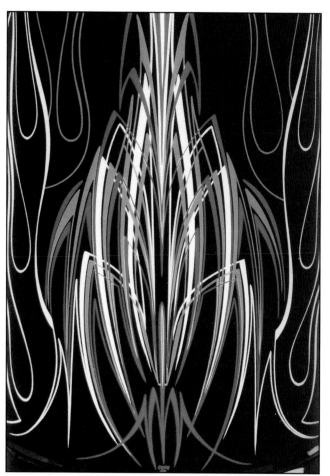
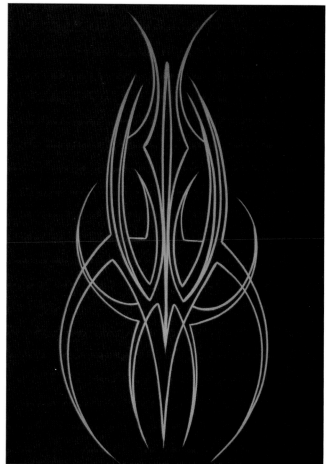

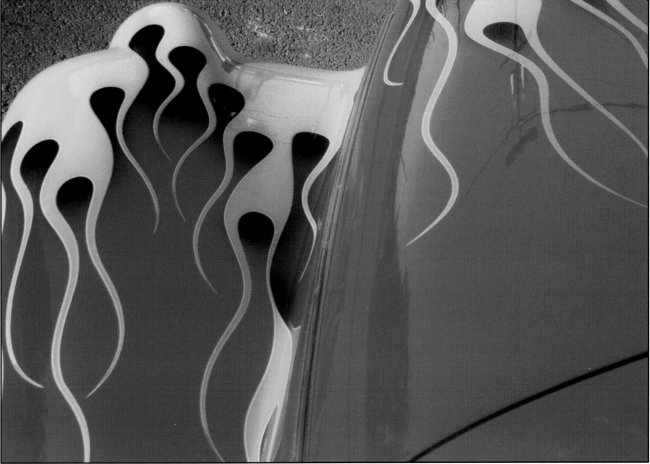

JOHN Hannukaine

SUPPLIES:

Paint Media: 1-Shot® lettering enamels
Brushes: Mack brushes
Other: Mineral spirits, Smoothie fish-eye eliminator, 1-Shot® hardener

At the age of 13, John Hannukaine discovered the pinstriping art of Jack Pudliner while vacationing with his aunt and uncle in Redding. At about the same time he saw Ed Roth's airbrushed shirt work in an issue of *Car Craft* magazine, and instantly became infatuated with the weirdo designs he saw. He bought a single-action Paasche airbrush, rigged it up to an old refrigerator compressor, and started painting like crazy.

Soon he discovered that people would actually pay for his striping and airbrush work. When he was old enough to drive, Hannukaine started working part time in a few different sign shops, managing to put himself through the University of Washington in the process. After graduating with an art education degree, Hannukaine served a two-year stint in the U.S. Navy as an illustrator/draftsman. (Just one of the things he and his friend Don King have in common.)

For the past 32 years, Hannukaine has operated a commercial sign and vehicle graphics business in Tumwater, Washington. He gives full credit to Bonnie, his wife of 37 years, who manages the books and raised their three children, Rachel, Adam and Alison.

Hannukaine, 60, has painted commercially for 46 years, and enjoys his craft today as much as he did in his youth, if not more. When asked about retirement, he answers, "I plan to paint as long as my creator blesses me with the ability to do so. After all, I hear tales of some people who retire to do what I've been able to do most of my life."

The Project:

This tutorial demonstrates how to achieve a blended effect in a short time using lettering enamels, a flat synthetic pictorial brush, and a small script detail brush.

Step 1

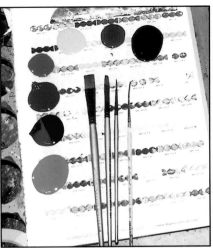

Step 2

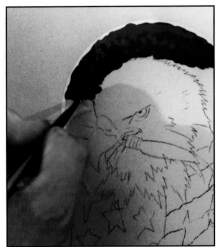

Step 3

Step 4

Step 5

Step 6

Step 1:
I started with a standard carbon paper to transfer the drawing to the panel's surface.

Step 2:
For illustration work like this, I pour the colors right onto the palette. Michael Lavallee's pictorial brushes by Mack, and a No. I American painter 4050 script brush are good tools. The I-Shot® lettering enamel is thinned with mineral spirits.

Step 3:
A circular shape in the background was painted with small crosshatch strokes blended from purple at the top to black on the bottom.

Step 4:
Starting with brilliant blue, I blended and transitioned the colors in the flag to process blue. All the strokes were down strokes.

Step 5:
This is the most important part of the project: blending from dark to light. Starting with pure brilliant blue, I painted a few strokes on the flag. Then, I went to the palette and added a little process blue to create a slightly lighter color. Painting a few strokes with this color, I continued by adding process blue, mixing and painting, and finished with pure process blue.

Step 6:
The same steps were repeated for the red and white sections of the flag. Note the blended flag colors. Don't try to blend too perfectly or you'll lose the hand-painted look.

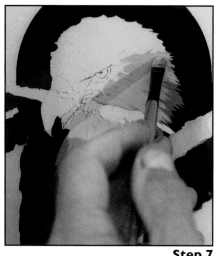
Step 7

Step 8

Step 9

Step 10

Step 11

Step 12

Step 7:
Working from dark to light again, I applied the feathers to the head, using quick strokes with the brush held sideways.

Step 8:
Here the feathers were painted from the darkest value to about the middle value. No waiting time was required between color changes, and everything was applied wet on wet.

Step 9:
The lightest strokes were applied here. Again, the brush was held on its side but this time in a flat position.

Step 10:
From dark to light, I painted in the beak and tongue, using small random and crosshatch strokes.

Step 11:
After the eye and brush were painted in, I detailed everything with a medium brown.

Step 12:
After adding paint and drips to the brush using Kansas City teal, I outlined everything with orange.

Step 13

Step 14

Step 15

Step 16

The Finished Piece

Step 13:
Building from dark to light, I highlighted the paint and drips with a lightened mixture of the teal.

Step 14:
The stars were painted with a slightly blue-tinted white, so they wouldn't overpower the blue.

Step 15:
The final shading was done with restoration clear mixed with a drop of black, and Smoothie brand fish-eye eliminator (approximately one drop per ounce). I used a soft brown quill to minimize the brush strokes.

Step 16:
The scroll striping here was done with a No. 3 4901 eclipse outliner from Dick Blick—the border stripe was done with a 00 Grumbacher striping brush.

The Finished Piece:
This project took about 90 minutes to 2 hours to complete.

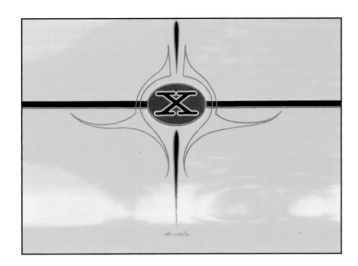

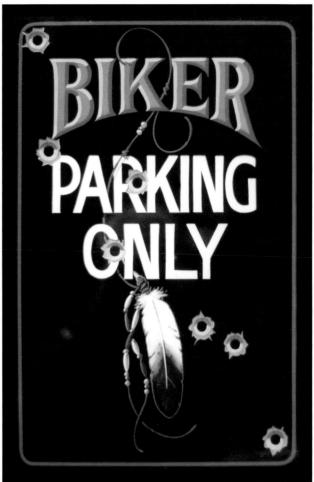

RICK Harris

SUPPLIES:

Paint Media: I-Shot® lettering enamels, House of Kolor® striping urethanes
Brushes: Hanover
Other: 3M™ tape

We all experience an event in life that changes everything, even if we don't realize it at the time. Rick Harris's came in the spring of 1969 when his father refused to co-sign a loan for a new Z-28 Camaro. Instead, Rick ended up with a new Volkswagen Beetle. He was 21 and wanted a muscle car, not a bug. So he took it home and pinstriped it. Proud of his work, he returned to the dealer to show the salesman what he had done, and was immediately hired to stripe another Beetle. Rick may not have known it then, but his father had done him a big favor.

By 1973 Harris was confident enough to stripe street rods at the Street Rod Nationals in Tulsa, Oklahoma. That's when he met pinstriping master Chuck Babbitt, or "Shaky Jake" as he was known in Southern California. By 1980 Harris pinstriped full time and made many trips to Costa Mesa to work with his mentor. Harris has been striping for more than 32 years, and says he still learns something new every day.

Step 1

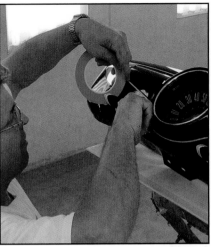

Step 2

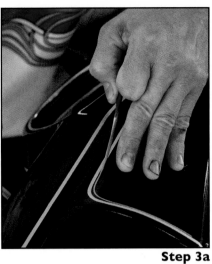

Step 3a

Step 3b

Step 4

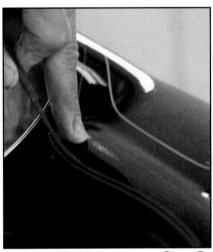

Step 5a

Step 1:
The first and most important step: I prepped the dash by thoroughly cleaning it with wax and grease remover.

Step 2:
I laid out the basic flow of the design with 3M™ 1/8-inch tape.

Step 3a & b:
Using the tape as a guide, I striped the first color, an apple green made by mixing a 50/50 ratio of 1-Shot® chrome yellow and emerald green. My brush of choice for this project was a #00 Hanover.

Step 4:
Continuing to use the tape as my guide, I used dark magenta for my next color.

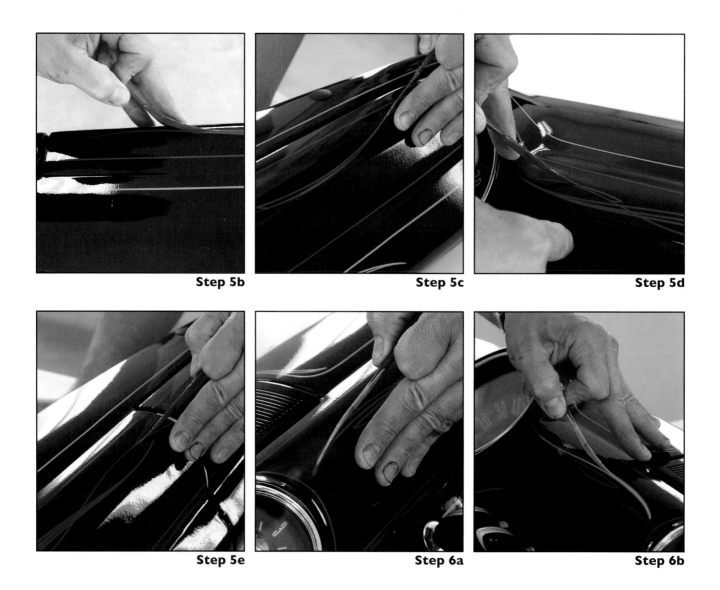

Step 5b   **Step 5c**   **Step 5d**

Step 5e   **Step 6a**   **Step 6b**

Step 5a, b, c, d, e:
Painting free-form, I filled the large empty spaces between
the lines with dark magenta.

Step 6a & b:
I filled in the connected "S" curves to add more weight to
the design.

Step 7a

Step 7b

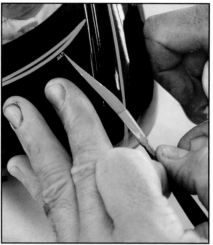

Step 8

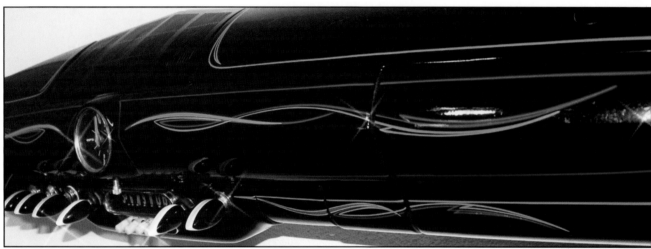

The Finished Piece

Step 7a & b:
I performed more free-form striping with the green, alongside the purple to finish off the designs.

Step 8:
The signature is an important element. Shaky Jake once advised me, "always sign your work and make it smaller than a dime." This is a mark of pride and the best form of advertising.

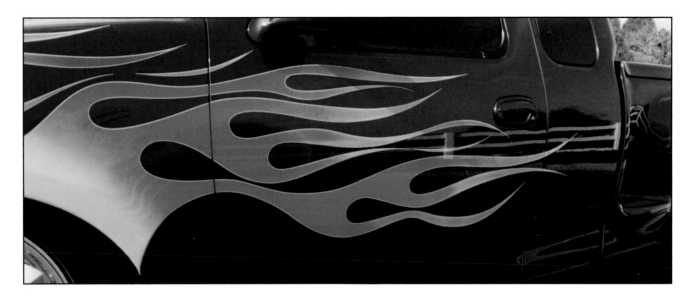

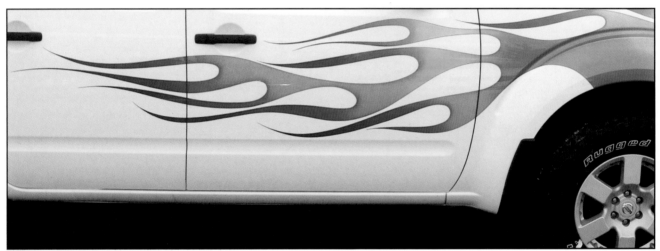

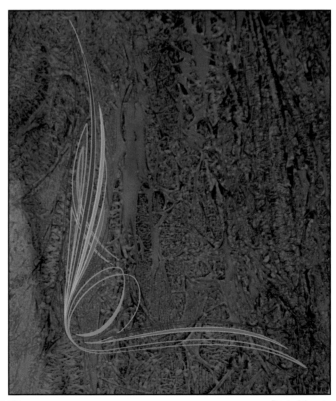

DAVID *Hightower*

SUPPLIES:
Paint Media: 1-Shot® lettering enamels
Brushes: Mack 000 Series 10, Mack Hannukaine quill, Mack 4042 Fitch, Liquitex Script 593, Silverwhite No. 4
Other: Stabilo pencil, Bon Ami cleaner

David Hightower earned a bachelor's degree in fine arts from his hometown school, Pittsburg State University in Kansas, and began his career as a sign painter in Chicago in 1966. But his love affair with striping actually began in 1957 when he read an article in *Rodding & Restyling* by Andy Southard Jr.

In 1991 David took five panels to Bloomington, Illinois, where he received raves from fellow letterheads. A year later he was in Canonsburg, Pennsylvania for the formation of the Pinheads, a group of more than a dozen professional stripers.

David counts among his influences Southard, Von Dutch and Dean Jefferies. He credits King George II of Lawrence, Kansas, with helping him with designs, and in shaping his pinstriping philosophy. The letterhead movement, especially the work of Alton Gillespie and Glen Weisgerber, has also inspired him.

Panel photos by Teresa Holman.

Step 1

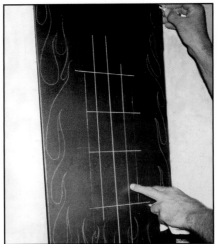

Step 2

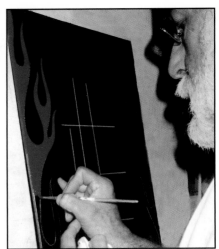

Step 3

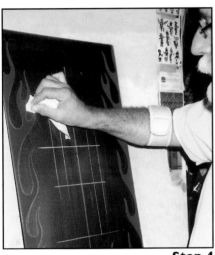

Step 4

Step 5

Step 6

Step 1:
For design symmetry and accuracy, I drew a grid with a Stabilo pencil and ruler.

Step 2:
With the Stabilo, I laid out a set of flames for the border.

Step 3:
I filled in the flames with red using a Liquitex Kolinsky Plus Script 593 brush.

Step 4:
After the red dried, I cleaned off the Stabilo lines with Bon Ami on a cloth.

Step 5:
I then added orange to the inside of the flames, applying the paint smoothly, trying to avoid the look of heavy brushstrokes.

Step 6:
I paletted the brush for the next step.

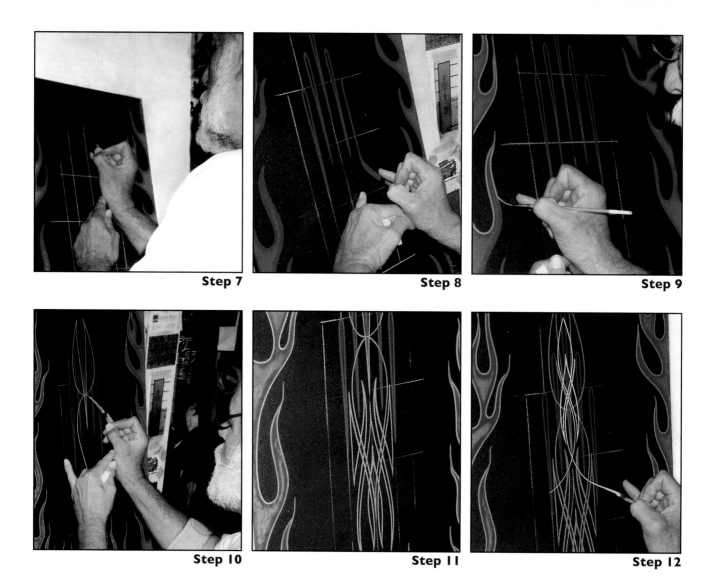

Step 7

Step 8

Step 9

Step 10

Step 11

Step 12

Step 7:
Notice how my left hand keeps the right one steady.

Step 8:
Teardrops inspired by Tommy the Greek are a favorite. A newer or "fatter" brush works best for teardrops, accomplished best in one stroke with no touch-ups.

Step 9:
I outlined the flames with a Silverwhite No. 4 brush, which is better for cornering than long lines.

Step 10:
A 000 Mack Series 10 brush was used for this phase of design work.

Step 11:
I completed the main stripe design and achieved a good balance.

Step 12:
I used white—an extremely contrasting color—sparingly to give the design a real punch. With white, less is more.

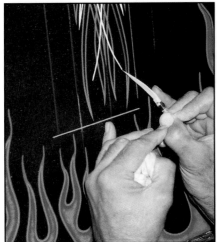

Step 13a

Step 13b

Step 13:

I extended the design downward, ending it in a teardrop just past the purple and leaving enough room for a signature. The job is complete.

The Finished Piece

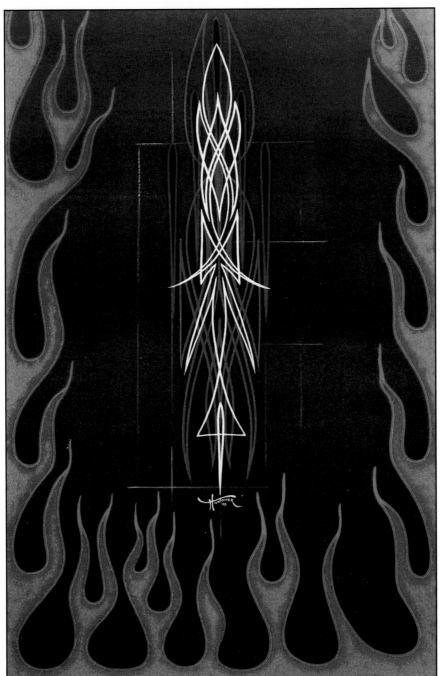

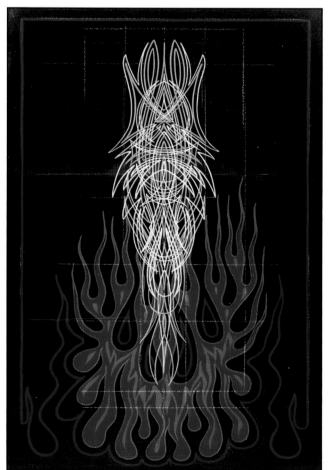

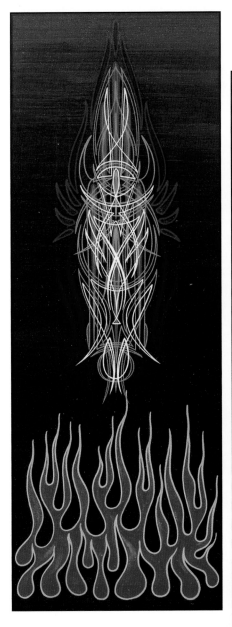

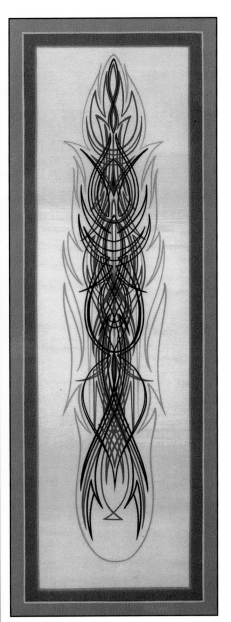

ART *Himsl*

SUPPLIES:

Paint Media: 1-Shot® lettering enamels
Brushes: Xcaliber 00 striping brush
Other: 1-Shot® 6001 low temperature reducer,
House of Kolor striping urethanes

Art Himsl's artwork transcends a particular era and style, and continues to explore the technical and creative boundaries of pinstriping. Many look to him for inspiration.

Calling his style "creative precision," Himsl's vision combines the impact of elegant lines and the use of dramatic color. Himsl's artwork has been published in many magazines, and exhibited in museums. Art's arsenal includes sprayguns, airbrushes, striping brushes, an English roll, and a wire-feed welder.

Art's best advice: "Paint all the time. Stay on top of the materials. You've got to pick up a brush and just start doing it!"

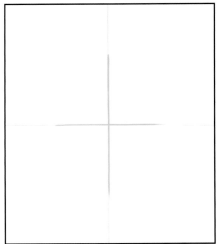

Step 1

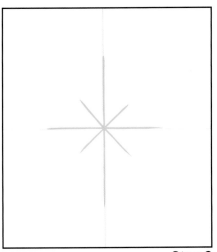

Step 2

Step 3

Step 4

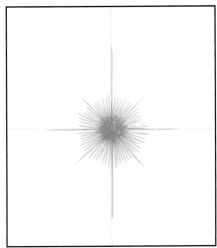

Step 5

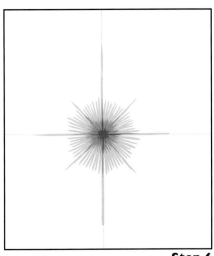

Step 6

Step 1:
After marking the centerline with a pencil, I began the starburst design by applying the first color, yellow, down and across the center.

Step 2:
I striped an "X" through the center using two strokes that are approximately half the length of the strokes in Step 1.

Step 3:
I added additional "X" strokes to build the center of the starburst.

Step 4:
I continued adding strokes until the design was filled in.

Step 5:
With orange, I added smaller strokes.

Step 6:
I finished the starburst with dark magenta in the center of the design.

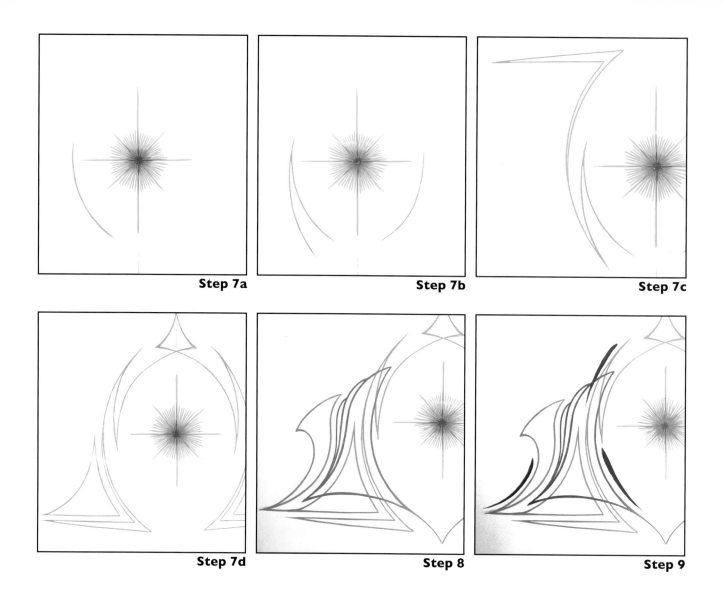

Step 7a   Step 7b   Step 7c

Step 7d   Step 8   Step 9

Step 7:
Using teal, I worked the design from left to right.

Step 8:
With the addition of process blue, the design takes form.

Step 9:
Teardrops were added with dark blue.

The Finished Piece: I added a stroke around the teardrops with small dots of teal and yellow, and signed my piece.

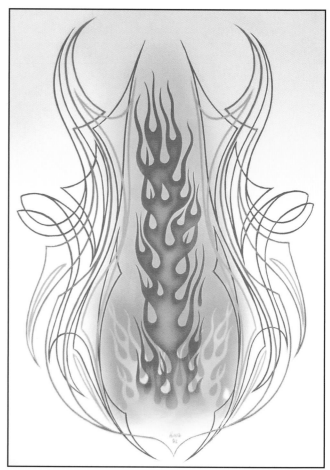

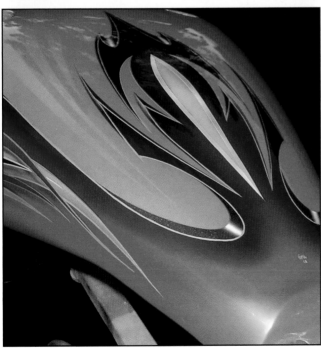

BOB *Iverson*

SUPPLIES:
Paint Media: House of Kolor® striping urethanes
Brushes: Mack Original Series 10 blue wrap, striping sword
Other: 1-Shot® quick dry gold size, hardener, PPG acrylic-clean DX 330, Sepp Leaf 23-karat gold leaf, cotton balls, velvet spinning tool

For as long as Bob Iverson can remember, art has been his passion. He didn't know a thing about striping until he saw the work of Shaky Jake and Phil Whetsone around his neighborhood beach area of Southern California. Interested, he finally worked up the nerve to ask Vince Bartelon, a buddy's dad, some questions. He advised, "Get a black-handle Grumbacher, in a 0 or 00, and some Sherwin Williams enamel. There's a store in Santa Ana." Iverson was 14 with no driver's license so his mother drove him to the art store. That purchase, made 31 years ago, changed his life.

For Iverson, every project has an element that can make it special. And there's profit to be made as well: "It's amazing how a little line can support a family," he says.

Iverson strives to make every project outstanding, and admires colleagues whose work graces this book. "They know who they are and they let their brush talk for them. I'm honored to be published with them and it is the number one reason I'm taking part in this book."

He says he will soon have a sign hanging in his shop that reads, "I'm having fun at your expense."

The Project:
Joe Curtes brought his Harley-Davidson-powered chopper to my shop, and the first thing I had to do was get him over the "I-wonder-what-the-hell-you're-going-to-do" jitters. So I told him, "You've seen my work, that's why you're here. I'll have some fun and you'll love it."

The concept is to accentuate the tallness of the West Coast Chopper's frame-and-tank combo. I'll work the design up the front of the tank, and down over the top. A 3-D effect will be created as the design moves around the tank and down under the bottom. The open-frame design lets me show off on both ends of the rear fender.

The tank and fender were base-coated in black by Rick Walker at Westcoast Colorworks in Huntington Beach, California. The frame was powder-coated and will be finished differently—not clear-coated—than the tank and fender.

Step 1

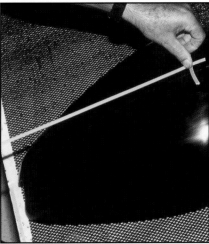
Step 2

Step 3

Step 4

Step 5

Step 6

Step 1:
I cleaned the black-based tank with PPG acrylic-clean DX 330. The can acted as a prop.

Step 2:
I located the center and laid down 1/4-inch tape. Then I ran a white Stabilo pencil along the edge of the tape, which I then removed. I did the same with the rear fender. You don't want to discover at the end that your design is off-center!

Step 3:
I strained 1-Shot® Quick Dry gold size into a non-wax paper cup, and added a drop of 1-Shot® imitation gold for visibility. I didn't use a catalyst in the size in order to prevent the gold leaf from wrinkling when clearcoated. I didn't mix the catalyst directly in the cup with the size; instead, I paletted it separately so that the cup-o-size didn't gum up in a matter of 10 minutes.

Step 4:
Using a lettering quill, I filled in the taped-off teardrop with size on the back fender. I did the same with the tank top and front.

Step 5:
I removed the tape and let the size set for about 30 to 50 minutes.

Step 6:
I tested the size by lightly dragging the back of my knuckle across the design. When you hear a "squeak" and see no visible smears, you can then apply the 23-karat leaf.

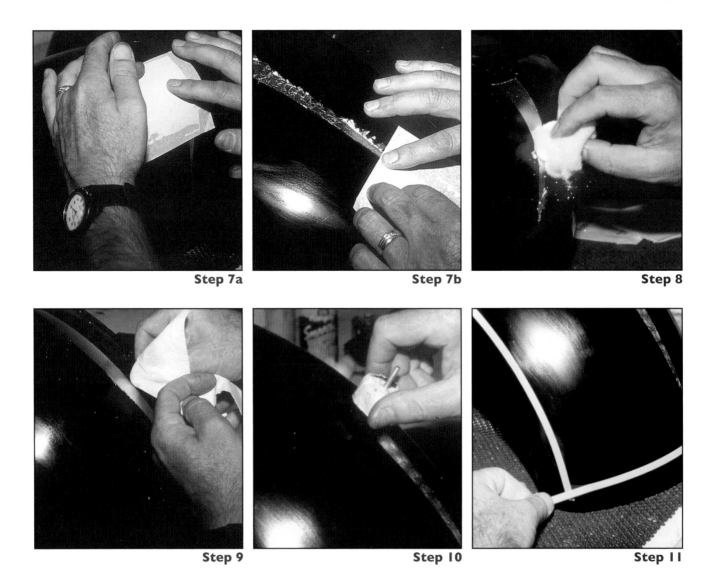

Step 7a   Step 7b   Step 8

Step 9   Step 10   Step 11

Step 7a & b:
I gently rubbed the patent 23-karat gold leaf over the areas with the size.

Step 8:
The excess gold was removed carefully with a cotton wad.

Step 9:
Some of the gold is so sensitive to adhesion it has a tendency to stick to the base or even a fingerprint. A clean towel and some DX 330 will remove any excess gold.

Step 10:
After an hour or so, the size should be hard enough to twist a machine turn into the gold. If you spin too soon, it's easy to burn through the leaf. This spinner or spinning tool was made from a piece of velvet wrapped over a cotton wad. A 3/4-inch to one-inch diameter chunk works well. This process adds a glitzy look that is sure to elicit lots of "oohs" and "aahs."

Step 11:
After allowing the leafed set to dry overnight, I used 1/4-inch tape to lay out a boundary line on the fender.

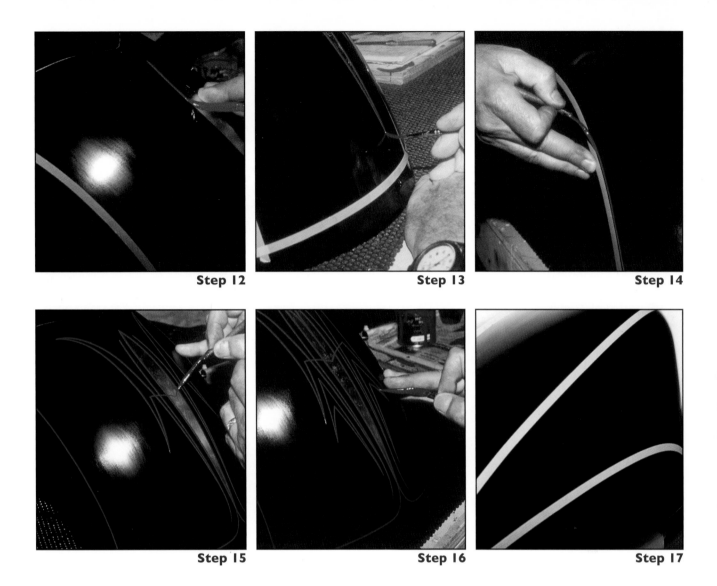

Step 12   Step 13   Step 14

Step 15   Step 16   Step 17

Step 12:
I fitted the fender and seat into the frame, and marked where the seat lies on the fender with a Stabilo pencil to keep the design from going under the seat. I laid out the design with House of Kolor Roman Red striping urethane. The Roman Red looks great on black, and is reminiscent of the old-school style.

Step 13:
The center design was tied into the boundary stripe at this point. I used an Alan Johnson signature Mack brush to do the radius. The actual turn came later.

Step 14:
I moved around the fender stripe using a Mack Original Series 10 blue wrap brush.

Step 15:
Despite the teardrop leaf layout, a secondary concern is to show off the seat shape. With that in mind, I moved up some of the stripe design to echo and accentuate the shape. I worked with both hands to get maximum comfort as each line went on. Striping over the leaf with urethane is unforgiving. If you try to remove it, the gold will smudge and re-leafing will be in order. Note that there was no intercoat clear over this black base — allowing for no mistakes. (Can you hear Rick Walker snickering?)

Step 16:
I continued to build the design. That's a wrap for the back of the fender.

Step 17:
The West Coast Chopper tank is tall, and I wanted the design to accentuate that. With 1/4-inch tape I laid out a design where the bottom tape swoops forward and down with the top, incorporating the tank's front design.

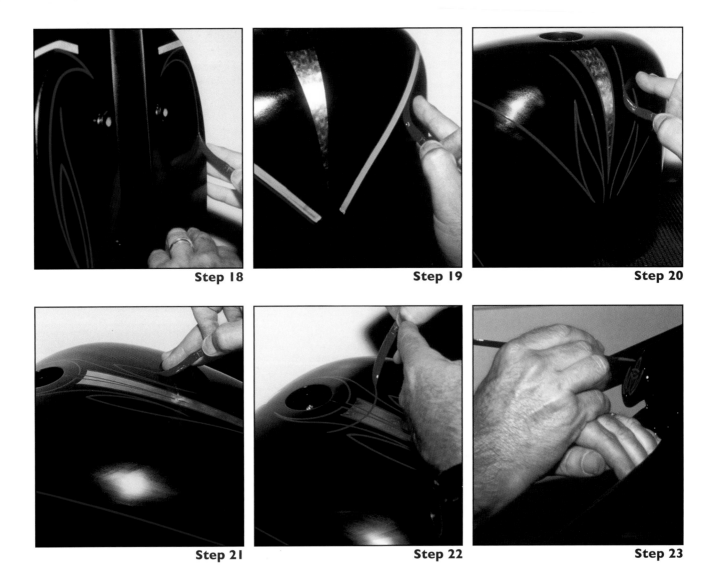

Step 18

Step 19

Step 20

Step 21

Step 22

Step 23

Step 18:
The tank bottom was striped first. I started on the left side, then to the right.

Step 19:
I laid the tank down to stripe the sideline back so that it met the top line seen in the next shot.

Step 20:
Here again the tallness of the tank was emphasized. Keep your fingers out of the paint. These are foundation lines and they must be right.

Step 21:
I worked the top of the tank next, paying careful attention over the leaf. This layout helped visually lengthen the tank's top. The engine turn in the gold is, as some of your younger customers might say, "disgustingly epic."

Step 22:
Oh Baby...radius over the leaf and the job is almost done.

Step 23:
A mini design on the dorsal tube of the frame (a small spot at the front of the seat) and it's ready for clearcoating.

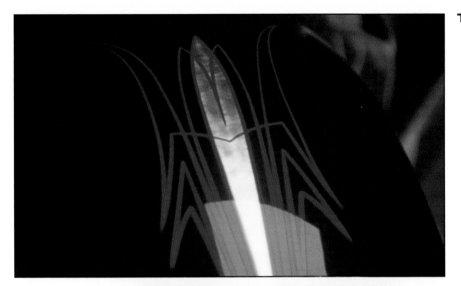

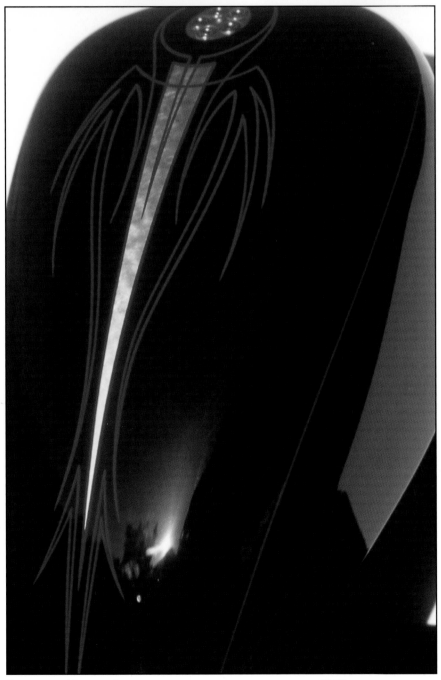

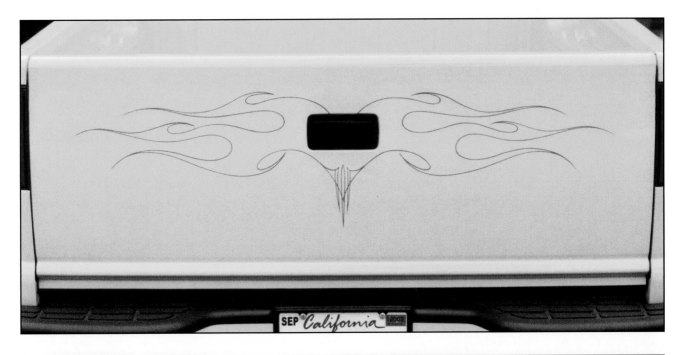

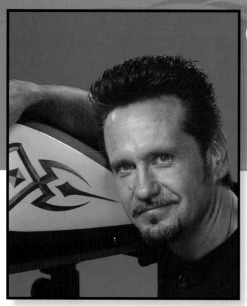

GARY *Jenson*

SUPPLIES:
Paint Media: 1-Shot® lettering enamels
Brushes: Jenson's Swirly Q JS2
Other: 1-Shot® 601 reducer

Gary Jenson became intrigued by pinstriping as a child, and his interest never faded. By his early 20s, Gary decided to dedicate his life to the craft. And when Jenson's pleas for instruction from well-known area artists were met with rejection, he became determined to learn on his own.

Through his talent and determination to excel in the art, Gary mastered pinstriping and the Buegler striping tool, for which he is considered one of the world's fastest and best.

After a couple of years as a mobile striper, Jenson opened a shop in Salt Lake City, Utah, and has been going strong for more than 20 years. Jenson's Pinstriping attracts mostly vehicle projects for pinstriping, lettering, graphics, and many gold leaf jobs.

Gary's love of pinstriping also extends to his involvement in promoting the craft. He even hosted the famed Annual Brush Bash for nearly 10 years.

By the mid 1990s Jenson's talent for scroll style striping was nationally recognized. As a result, MACK Brush Company commissioned Gary to create the highly popular Jenson's Swirly-Q series of striping brushes.

Perhaps Gary's greatest strengths as a striper are his willingness to share his knowledge with others through teaching events, and his accessibility to anyone who calls. In fact, Jenson is a head instructor for the prestigious and internationally known Airbrush Getaway Professional Workshop Program (www.airbrushaction.com).

His exceptional how-to DVDs, produced by *Airbrush Action Magazine*, include *Vehicle Goldleafing Techniques*, *Buegler Mastery* and *Pinstriping Dynamics*.

A MACK Pinstripers Hall of Fame inductee, Jenson remains committed to making pinstriping his life and passion.

Step 1

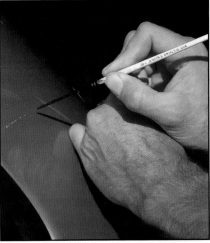

Step 2a

Step 2b

Step 3

Step 4

Step 1:

For this project, I used a Jenson's Swirly Q JS2 scroll brush. Because the paint needs to be reduced more for this type of striping, faster drying 1-Shot® 601 works well for thinning. I thin the paint just enough to work with, but not too "drippy." Loading the brush is a critical part of scrolling, so I dipped the brush up to its heel, then worked the paint into the brush by using the inside of the cup as a palette, patting one side of the brush and then rotating it. I lightly run the brush over the edge of the cup, removing any excess paint, and begin the scrollwork on my substrate as quickly as possible.

Step 2:

Hand positioning and brush technique for scrolling are simple to master. Use the same position and movements you'd use as if drawing the design with a pencil. Do not twirl the brush to make loops.

When scrolling, keep the brush perpendicular to the surface to ensure even paint distribution. If you hold the brush at an angle, the bristles will flop over halfway

through your first circle. To steady your hand and avoid contact with the design, use either the hand-over-hand method (2a) or the pinkie-down method (2b).

Step 3:

The best practice exercise for scroll striping is to render a series of continuous loops. To practice symmetry, work left to right, and then work right to left. (If your brush is loaded correctly, you should be able to continue the loops for about 10 inches without reloading.) Once you feel comfortable with the flow of the brush strokes, you're ready to practice the actual scrolls.

Step 4:

"Leaves" are a scroll's finishing touch, and I generally use two types. The first type is a leaf whose bandwidth goes from thick to thin, starting with a "flood stroke." I push the brush hard at first, then ease up on the pressure. I twist the brush slightly at the end of the stroke to create a tapered effect.

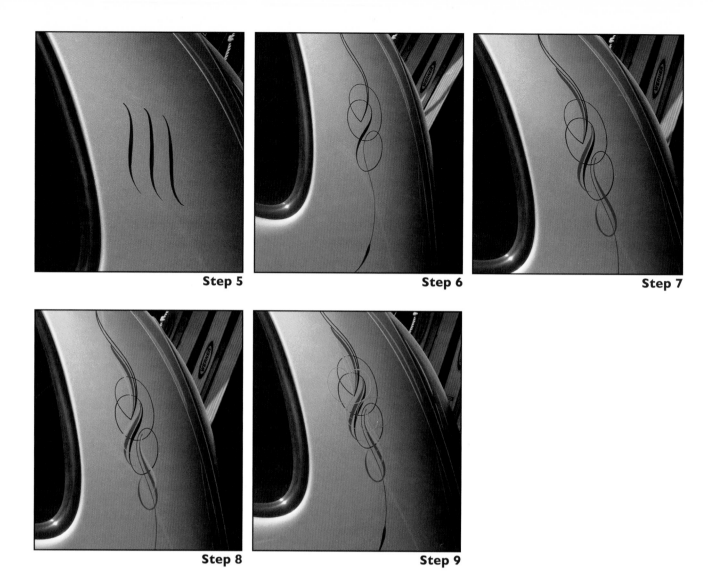

Step 5   **Step 6**   **Step 7**

Step 8   **Step 9**

Step 5:
The second type of leaf's bandwidth goes from thin to thick, to thin again. To render this leaf, load less paint in your brush and palette the tip of the brush into a point. Start the stroke with light pressure, and while pulling down, add more pressure until you achieve the desired width. Continue pulling down, decreasing bandwidth by decreasing the pressure. Slightly twist the brush at the end of the stroke to create a tapered end.

Step 6:
Make the base of the scroll design implementing the same techniques you used when practicing loops. Remember: Hold your brush perpendicular to the surface, use the hand-over-hand or pinkie-down method to keep your hand steady, and don't twist the brush during this phase of the design. If you're still having trouble, you may want to check if your paint consistency is too thick or too thin.

Step 7:
At this point, you can start adding leaves to the design.

Step 8:
As you add more leaves to the design, use colors that complement one another.

Step 9:
The last color is added and the project is finished.

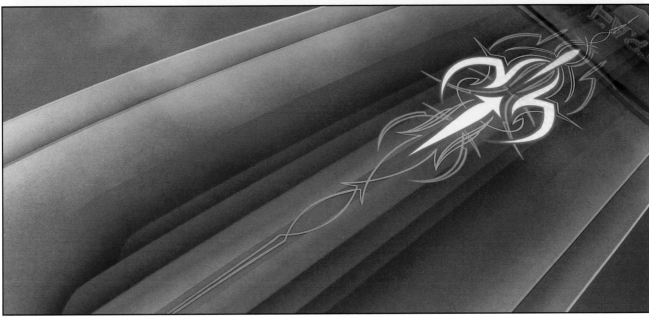

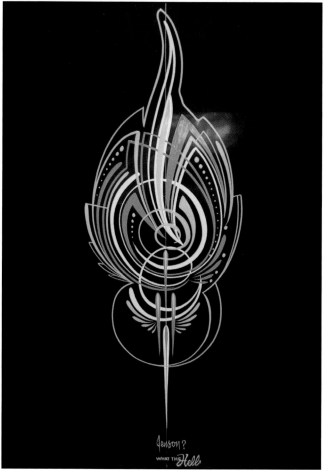

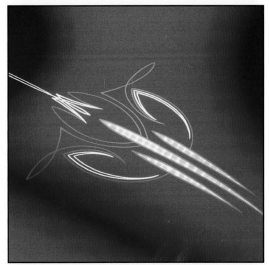

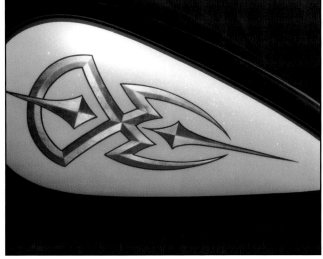

DON *King*

SUPPLIES:

Paint Media: 1-Shot® lettering enamels, Wunda size, urethane topcoat
Brushes: Xcaliber #0 striping brush
Other: 23-carat August Ruhl patent gold, velveteen, cotton, Grifhold 113-B swivel knife, Gerber backing, 230 vinyl

Don King was born and raised in the small town of Kelso, Washington, a real hot-rod town where he developed a lifelong passion for cars and their designs. Influenced by the automotive art he saw in magazines of the time, King as a young boy was always drawing pictures of cars and graphics (most often in geometry class). He was constantly told that he would never amount to anything if he didn't stop drawing. As early as junior high school he was airbrushing T-shirts with Roth-type designs, and in high school, after striping his 1938 Chevy Coupe, he began striping all his friends' rides.

In 1964, the self-taught artist entered the U.S. Navy's illustrator-draftsman school before serving on the USS Kitty Hawk and later, the USS Enterprise, for a guided tour of Vietnam and the South China Sea. Upon returning home, King worked for Boeing as an illustrator. Then, he joined an electric-sign company as a designer/sign painter.

Eight years later he and a group of partners started their own electric-sign company. As part of the sign-making business, King embraced the computer as another tool for his toolbox, but never divorced himself from hand-drawn art, continuing his striping and hand-lettering work during evenings and weekends. After 19 years in the partnership, King, on his 49th birthday, walked away and started his own business. His solo venture, King Grafix, does everything from signs and corporate logos to vehicle lettering and graphics, pinstriping and cartoons.

Another career turning point came when King purchased John Hannukaine's book, *Pinstriping and Vehicle Graphics,* at a car show. After introducing himself to the author, King was invited by Hannukaine to a Pinheads get-together. King was hooked. After so many years of working alone and enduring so much trial and error, he

had finally found a place where fellow artists could share ideas, techniques and camaraderie. Since that day, King has attended events all over the country, meeting and becoming friends with some of the best talents in the profession.

King has a simple design philosophy: A design isn't complete when you can't add more to it, but rather when you can't take anything away. Know when to quit.

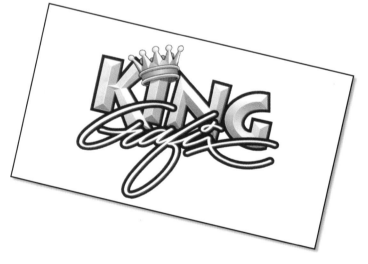

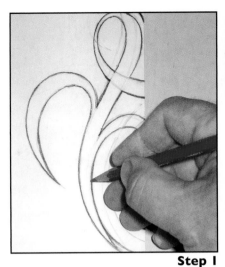

Step 1

Step 2

Step 3

Step 4

Step 5

Step 6

Step 1:
I drew half of the design on a piece of paper.

Step 2:
I scanned the drawing into the computer and redrew the curves and mirror image. Then I added center and segment lines. For this project the layout was an inch-and a-half too short for proper balance, but a few keystrokes achieved the necessary change.

Step 3:
Typically, you should always print several copies of the design for multiple use, because each copy is virtually destroyed after cutting.

Step 4:
After cutting out the design on Gerber Mask, I weeded, applied transfer tape, and transferred the design to a clean panel surface.

Step 5:
Speed is very important in this step. I applied water-based Wunda gold size to the design using a soft watercolor brush. The sizing goes on white, turns lavender, and then dries to clear.

Step 6:
I removed the masking immediately before it totally dried, and cleaned up any sizing that had bled under the masking with a damp paper towel of denatured alcohol.

Step 7

Step 8

Step 9

Step 10

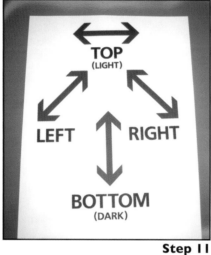

Step 11

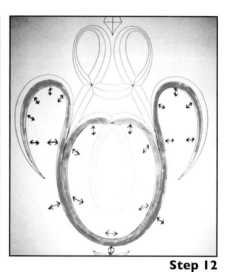

Step 12

Step 7:
I applied 23-carat patent gold, and rubbed it down using the backing paper. I prefer using August Ruhl gold because it burnishes extremely well.

Step 8:
I removed the excess gold with soft cotton.

Step 9:
The design was ready for burnishing.

Step 10:
Using a copy of the layout, I cut segment templates with my Grifhold 113-B swivel knife from the backing sheet of Gerber 230 vinyl (it's sturdy, transparent and free).
I usually cut them as I go in order to keep confusion to a minimum.

Step 11:
This is my directional chart for burnishing. Burnishing in different directions causes light reflection to give the illusion of shapes and bevels.

Step 12:
This photo shows a burnishing plan for two of the segments, horizontal being the lightest to vertical being the darkest.

Step 13

Step 14

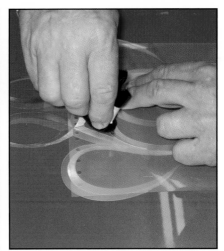

Step 15

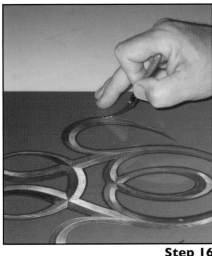

Step 16

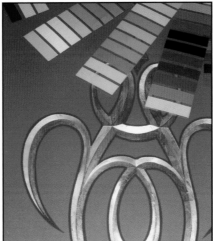

Step 17

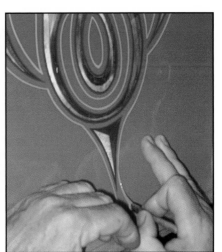

Step 18

Step 13:
I used a burnishing tool made from velveteen (imitation velvet available at fabric stores) wrapped around cotton.

Step 14:
I placed a template over the segment to be burnished.

Step 15:
I burnished in the direction needed to achieve the effect. Light pressure is all that is needed—don't overdo it.

Step 16:
After I had clearcoated with a urethane topcoat that's slightly overlapped onto the background, I outlined the design with 1-Shot® maroon on a #00 Xcaliber striping brush.

Step 17:
Color samples from a Gerber vinyl chart are one of my favorite tools for helping to decide on colors. Sometimes I discover color combinations that I might never have thought of.

Step 18:
Using a mixed pale orange of 1-Shot®, I striped a second outline.

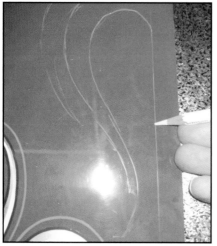

Step 19

Step 20

Step 19:
My designs just evolve, and this one needed some fill in the corners for balance. I laid out a flame lick and border, using a white china marker.

Step 20:
Using the same maroon as on the first outline, I striped the border.

The Finished Piece:
After drying and clean-up, the panel is ready to hang on the wall.

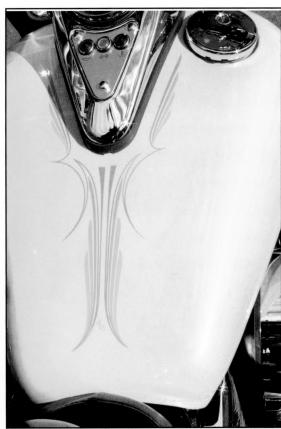

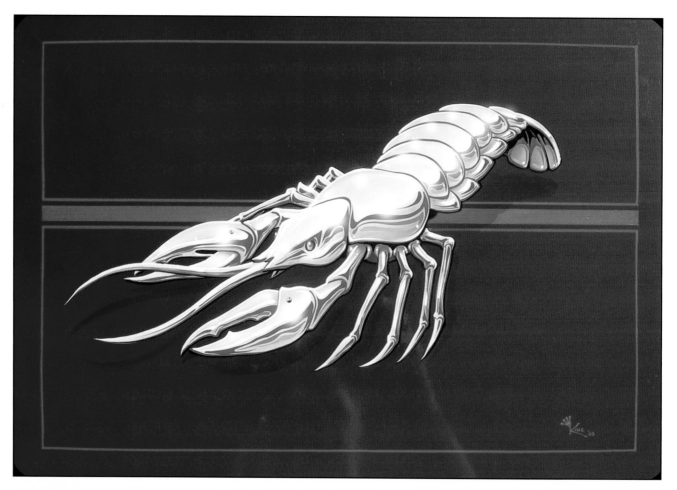

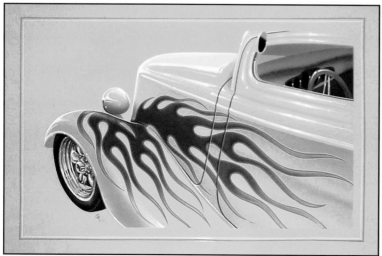

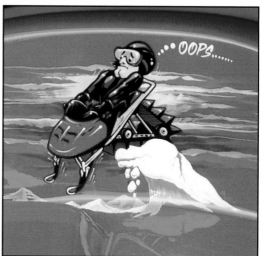

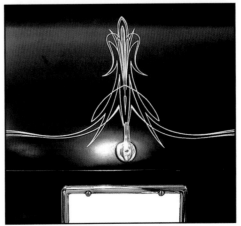

KEITH *Knecht*

SUPPLIES:

Paint Media: 1-Shot® Lettering Enamels
Brushes: Mack Brushes #000 10 series
Other: Mahl stick, 3M™ rubber squeegee

Keith Knecht began learning the fundamentals of pinstriping in 1955 from Ed Gaston, an old factory-line striper at Stutz, Reo, and finally at Willy's Overland, in Toledo, Ohio. Working with Gaston, who was born in the 1800s and learned the trade in St. Louis, Missouri, helped Knecht gain knowledge from someone with historic experience.

Among the lessons Knecht learned was the importance of knowing the proper brush for each job. For 49 years, Knecht has been using Mack brushes, and he believes they fit every need—the 10 series for fancy designs, the 000 for long straight lines, and the new striper based on the old Grumbacher brush. He also uses a Mahl stick for designs that require better control.

Knecht is willing to share his knowledge: "A brush is such a personal tool. Each painter breaks in a brush differently, so what works for me won't work for another striper and vice versa. The real secret to becoming a good pinstriper is no secret at all—it's practice, practice, practice."

Knecht says getting paint to work just right is a function of experience and experimentation. Getting to know which additives—boiled linseed oil, kerosene and "Penetrol"—to use under various conditions is also key. He advises using a 3M™ rubber squeegee for the clean-up, and a rotary mini-lift that can raise a low-slung vehicle at least 30 inches.

His career and life philosophy: "What I do is what I am. You can never pay someone who teaches you something,

but when you gain that knowledge, you accept the obligation to pass it on."

He also likes to quote Winston Churchill: "It's not the end, it's not even the beginning of the end, but it is the end of the beginning!"

Step 1

Step 2

Step 3

Step 4

Step 5

Step 6

Step 1:
I adjusted the height, length, and tilt with the balancer.

Step 2:
I placed the wheel on the unit.

Step 3:
I screwed the striping arm onto the cap.

Step 4:
After setting the proper placement, I striped the ivory line by turning the wheel with my left hand.

Step 5:
Spinning the wheel with my left hand, I continued striping the ivory line, making sure my right hand is held firmly to the guide and the brush doesn't move.

Step 6:
I finished the wheel with two wide orange stripes and two narrow ivory stripes.

Reinventing the Wheel
By Keith Knecht

Pinstripers go back eons. Back in the days when people lived in caves, some guy painted pictures on his walls, probably because he thought it made the cave more homey.

Then someone invented the wheel and things really got interesting. Wagons, buggies, coaches and trolley cars had to be decorated. And when the motor car came along—well, let's just say pinstriping made an evolutionary leap. It was only natural that pinstripers would see the automobile as a new opportunity to express themselves.

One of the more unusual avenues of expression is presented by the wheel itself. Over the past 48 years, I've been called upon more than once to pinstripe wheels—wagon wheels, wood-spoke wheels, and steel wheels for circa-1930s, 1940s and 1950s autos.

But I never looked forward to striping those steel wheels. Some could have as many as five lines each. Walking backward that much only made me dizzy, and I'm already dizzy enough. I knew there had to be a better way, and when I encountered an old tri-base wheel-balancer, the light bulb went on: Maybe it could be modified for striping wheels.

Tom Hilding, my mechanic, gave me this old wheel balancer. I drew a few rough sketches and took them and the balancer to Larry Latimore. He looked at the drawings and said, "I see what you want. Just leave it and I'll call you when it's done." When I saw what he had done, I couldn't have been more pleased.

So far it's working fine. I just sit on my stool, set the adjustable arm, load my brush, and turn the wheel with my left hand. My next move is to add an electric motor with a clutch pedal geared to about 2 miles per hour. That will be my winter project.

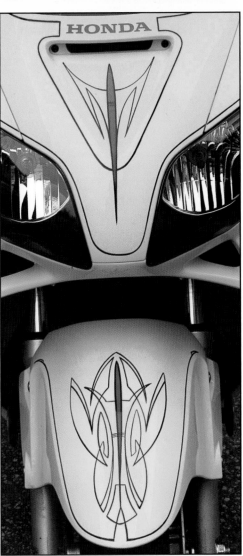

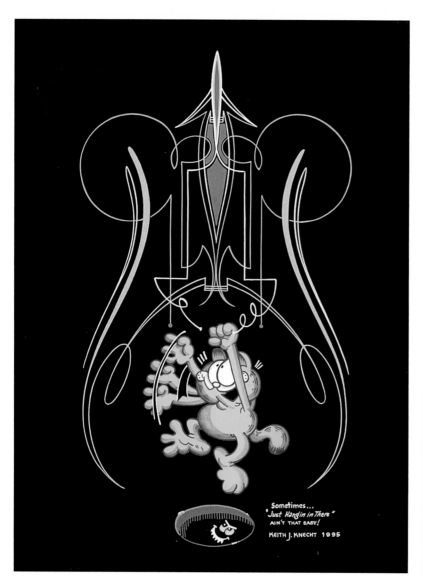

GARY *Kupfer*

SUPPLIES:

Paint Media: 1-Shot® lettering enamels, Sikkens Autobase & Autonova

Brushes: Grumbacher 1020 #00-4, Xcaliber #0000-000, Cosmos #0-1, Hanover LTD #0, Lowe Cornwell #2, Alan Johnson liners, Dick Blick Eclipse #1, Kafka #3 (trimmed), daVinci #s 1-2

Other: Paasche VL airbrush, Scotch Masking & Magic tape, Sherwin Williams surface cleaner, automotive lacquer thinner

A bachelor's of fine arts graduate of Manhattan's School of Visual Arts, Gary Kupfer has turned his full attention to automotive fine art, where his paintings hang in public and private collections.

Gary's moniker, "The Local Brush" comes from *Hot Rod* and *Hi Performance Car* magazines, which, along with many other titles, have featured Kupfer's work. In fact, his creations have graced the covers of more than 25 national car and motorcycle magazines since the mid-1960s. More recently, *Autoweek* magazine devoted five pages to Kupfer's teachings at the Center for Automotive Arts & Refinishing.

Among other Kupfer collectibles are the national award-winning show cars and motorcycles he built, as well as the classic Baldwin-Motion Camaros and Corvettes of the 1960s and 1970s he restyled and painted. These models are now made in miniature, with Kupfer's signature on many of them.

On his passion for the creative process and artistic challenges, Kupfer explained, "The cutting edge is not enough for me. I try to hover above the rest by creating what has not been done before. We all can copy, but if you're going to copy, it had better be better than the original or it's not worth copying."

Step 1

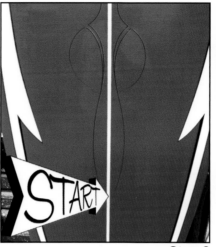

Step 2

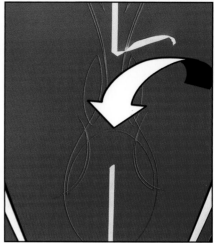

Step 3

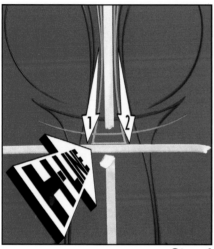

Step 4

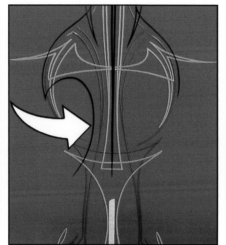

Step 5

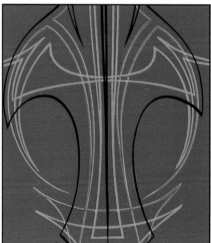

Step 6

Step 1:
The subject was a red surfboard on which I had already finished the lettering.

Step 2:
To start, I established a centerline as a guide, using 1/4-inch masking tape.

Step 3:
I broke the tape when I needed to allow for crossover lines.

Step 4:
Urethane paint with a hardener dries quickly, so I taped over it immediately to create a horizontal guide. I brought down the number 1 line and then the number 2 line, and used the horizontal line as a guide to connect them.

Step 5:
The black lines were used in keeping with the overall shape. They do not always have to cross over existing lines.

Step 6:
The overall shape of the design was very important, and it had to be pleasing to the eye. Fluidity in the work was key. Some lines should have a continuous, almost sexy, flow from top to bottom, not always spiked in an irrational manner.

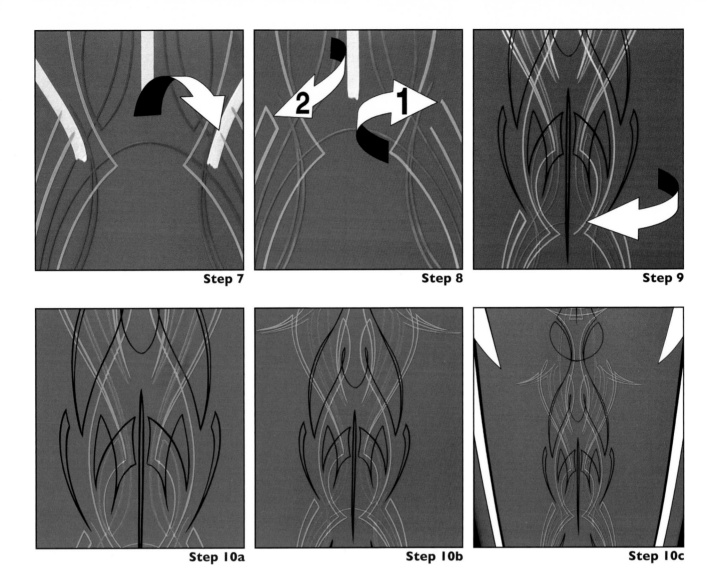

Step 7

Step 8

Step 9

Step 10a

Step 10b

Step 10c

Step 7:
To create a sharp and clean 90-degree change of direction, I pressed down a 1/4-inch tape using my fingernail. The paint will not penetrate beneath the tape. Overlap the tape with your stroke.

Step 8:
I removed the tape to expose the clean, sharp edge, and then connected the two lines.

Step 9:
I continued the lime-green line, matching stroke for stroke on each side of the design. Do not get too far ahead of yourself from one side to the other; if you do, it will make the job much harder.

Step 10a, b & c:
In these close-ups you can see the detail of the lines and the fluid movement I referred to.

The Finished Piece: Here is the overall design as well as the extra airbrush work and lettering that I did on the board. Now we're ready for the beach!

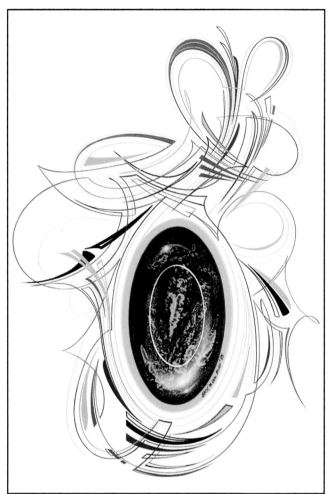

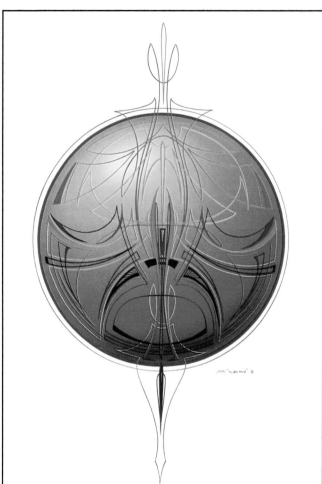

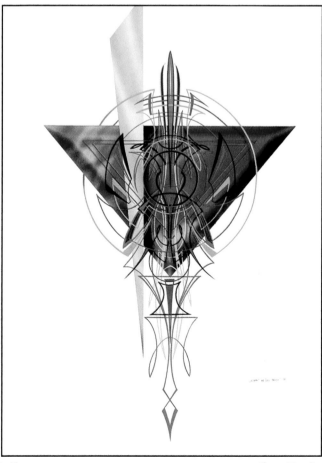

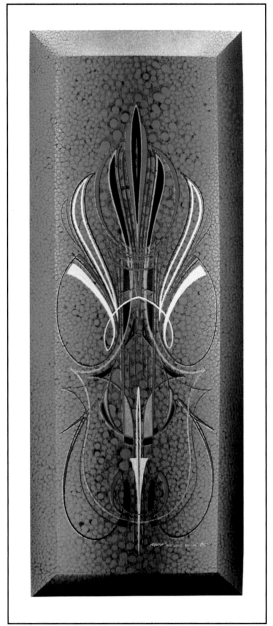

Gary Kupfer

RODY Kuschnereit

SUPPLIES:
Paint Media: 1-Shot® lettering enamels
Brushes: Hanover #1 brush

I grew up in Dodge City, Kansas in the 1950s. Dodge City was not the greatest car town in the country, but it did have a small custom shop owned by Dave Parks. Whenever I got a chance, I'd go there to check out the cool cars Dave was working on.

When I was 12, we moved to Wichita, Kansas, and one day a buddy of mine suggested we ride our bikes to Daryl Starbird's and Dave Stucky's shops. I became hooked on cars forever. After high school I became friends with Eldon Titus, who was just getting started doing some custom work. I'd hang around him, trying to learn as much as I could.

I started painting cars on the side, and then one day my wife Connie and I decided to leave Kansas. We moved to Aztec, New Mexico and I opened a body shop. I did some custom painting and tried pinstriping some of the jobs. I had no one to point me in the right direction, so those first few jobs weren't exactly masterpieces. Then, in 1975 I met Butch Tucker at a car show in Arizona. He striped my friend's 1937 Ford that I had flamed. My friend and I talked Butch into coming to Aztec and Durango for a couple of days to stripe some cars we'd lined up. That's when I got the pinstriping bug! Butch started giving me lessons and I practiced every night after work. When needed, I'd call Butch and tell him what was going wrong, and he'd troubleshoot the problem. The practicing and phone lessons with Butch eventually made me good enough to start charging.

In 1977 I was hired to manage a body shop in Denver. I striped cars in the evenings and weekends, slowly getting known around town. One day I got mad at work and quit. I went home and told Connie I was going to be a full-time

pinstriper. That was 27 years ago, and I've never regretted that decision. There were tough times, but you do what it takes to make things happen. Body shops and dealerships are my main clientele. I've striped more than 50,000 cars, trucks, motorcycles, and some things I would like to forget!

I look forward to teaching the trade to my grandson, Austin, who claims he's taking over when I get old and shaky. I hope to stripe another 15 years before that happens!

Special thanks to Butch Tucker, my great friend, for getting me started in this great profession. Butch, I hope I've made you proud!

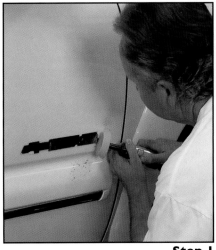

Step 1

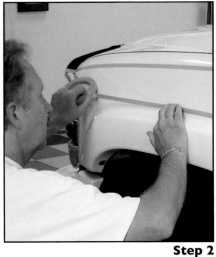

Step 2

Step 3a

Step 3b

Step 4a

Step 4b

Step 1:
I removed the name plates with a heat gun, and the tape residue with an air eraser made by 3M™. Then I cleaned the surface with wax and grease remover, followed by BONDO glass cleaner.

Step 2:
I laid out the basic design with green half-inch tape. I use the green variety because it's easier to see.

Step 3a & b:
I began on the right side, boxing in the first two panels on both fenders.

Step 4a & b:
Typically, I don't graph or layout the flames. I just study the vehicle and figure out where they should be placed, and I just go for it. Knowing the anatomy of flames helps greatly in this step.

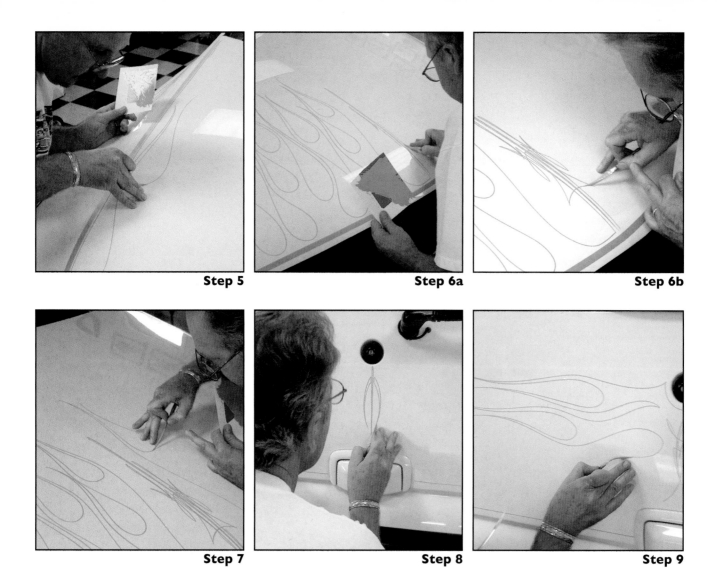

Step 5

Step 6a

Step 6b

Step 7

Step 8

Step 9

Step 5:
With both sides completed, I started on the right side of the hood and worked across.

Step 6a & b:
For this job I added a design to the center of the hood. I started with a teardrop and worked from there.

Step 7:
I continued the flames across the hood. They didn't have to be exactly the same as the ones on the right side, I just made sure there were the same number of licks. I try to keep them the same size and their tip lengths similar.

Step 8:
I started the design on the tailgate similar to the hood, with a tear drop, and worked from there. I don't graph a pattern because it's too time-consuming when doing production work.

Step 9:
I started the flames off of the design, painting the left side first, and then duplicating it on the right side.

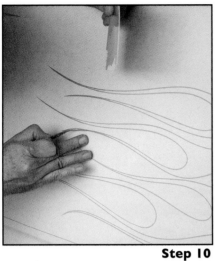

Step 10

Step 11

Step 10:
For light-colored cars, I darken the tips to give the flames more punch. For dark-colored cars, I lighten the tips.

Step 11:
I added all three colors to the hood, tailgate and pillar designs.

The Finished Piece:
Notice how pinstriped flames embellish the truck without it being too bold or overstated.

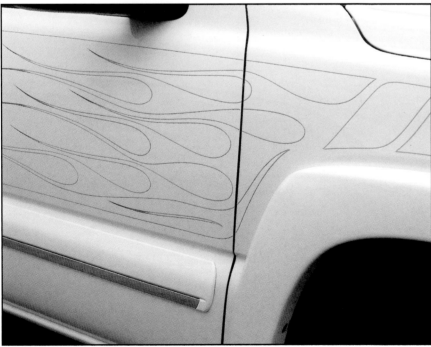

So You Want to Be a Pinstriper?
By Rody Kuschnereit

Always look for new ideas and ways to improve. You don't need to be a perfectionist, just be good at what you do. Anyone thinking of becoming a pinstriper for a living needs to learn how to draw a straight line first. If you don't master this basic ability, you don't stand a chance. The design work will come later. Study other stripers' styles; find something you like and copy it. After a while you'll start to add your own flare and develop your own style.

Look at every custom job you see and study it. You'll find some little stroke you can add to your style almost every time. No matter how long you stripe, there is always something to learn. Another thing you have to understand is the fine line between perfection and production. You have to be able to lay down a nice line quickly, not a perfect line that takes you all day to finish. A lot of people want names and initials done, but remember you don't have to learn to be a sign painter, just perfect a nice-looking script. If you have trouble keeping your line straight and spacing even, slightly rotate your brush as if you're steering it.

Ask some stripers you may know to give you any of their old brushes, and practice with those as much as you can. Don't run out to buy new brushes at first. I know you're going to think a new brush will solve all of your problems, but believe me, if that old brush worked for him, it'll work for you. And don't stripe in the sun or wind, always work inside so that your stripes will last longer.

Brush Preparation: I buy a year's supply of brush oil, and soak my brushes until I need them—a couple of months if possible! When you remove them from the oil, comb out the brush hairs with a toothbrush. Shorten or modify the brush handles to fit your hand better, slightly trim the tip of the brush to a square end, and just enough to remove any straggling hairs. I buy long-tapered brushes with the longest hairs.

Preparation: Wipe the surface with grease and wax remover, and then clean the area with BONDO glass cleaner to eliminate any static electricity. When your finger drags, it's clean enough. Lay down your tape guideline. I also use the tape as a measuring device, so make sure to stock up on various widths of tape. I stripe above or below the tape depending on what I need to do, and I always stripe the top line first. If the tape is on the bottom, I do the top line and then pull the tape to render the bottom because it's easier to see your spacing if the brush isn't in the way of your eyesight. Plus, it's easier to wipe off mistakes if you're working under the top line. I like using a palette consisting of a 4x6 coated cardstock. Ask your local print shop to cut up some misprints. I mix Edge brand thinner with 50% 1-Shot® Reducer. Once you achieve a good consistency paletting your paint, you're ready to lay down a line.

Striping: First, take a deep breath, and then breathe slowly. This slows your heart rate, which helps you have a steady hand. Lay down your brush and start pulling. Lean forward with the weight on your front foot, and slowly and continuously walk backwards, moving your body—not just your arm—until you reach the end of the panel. If you stop, restart by laying your brush about three inches back on your line and slowly add pressure until you establish the same width. Keep pulling. When starting a door edge, apply the brush and slightly push it forward, and then start pulling. Always come back to the end and clean up your line by pulling the other way.

Matching Colors: This can be a real pain. You need to learn how to look at a color and really see what's in it. If you're doing body shop repair work, you must be able to match the color in two to three minutes! If the old stripes are too faded or just a strange mixture, it's probably faster and easier to just stripe the whole side. Wasting time is wasting money!

Troubleshooting: If your line is fat, the paint is either too thin or you applied too much pressure. If your line has jagged edges, the paint is too dry. Just keep trying until you conquer the same consistency every time.

The DO's of Pinstriping:
Driving something cool that you've striped really helps sell your work.
If you offer same-day service you'll run yourself ragged, so have your shops call the day ahead.
Dealerships want you to look presentable in the showroom, so always appear clean.
Maintain a positive attitude in the shops.
Always hang wet stripe signs on your jobs.
Provide discounts to the shop's employees.
I take care of accidents but not stupidity.

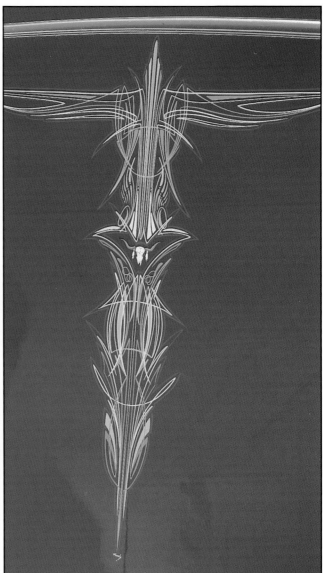

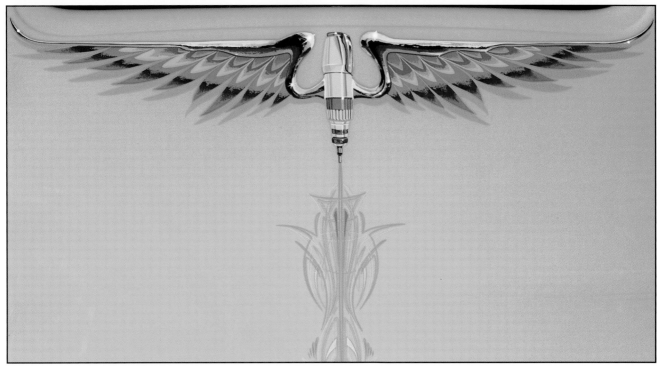

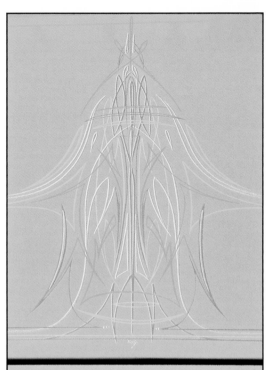

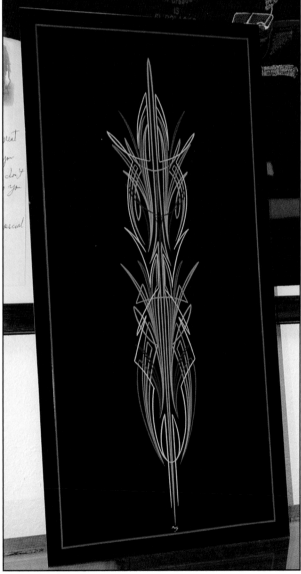

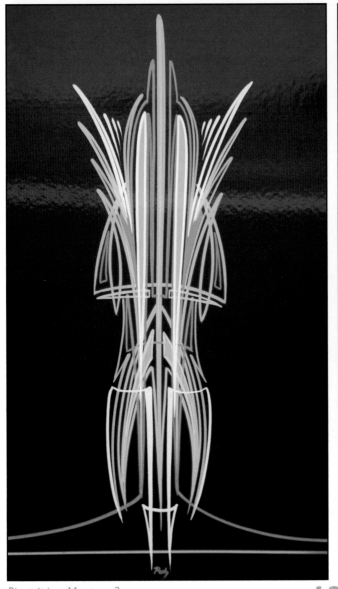

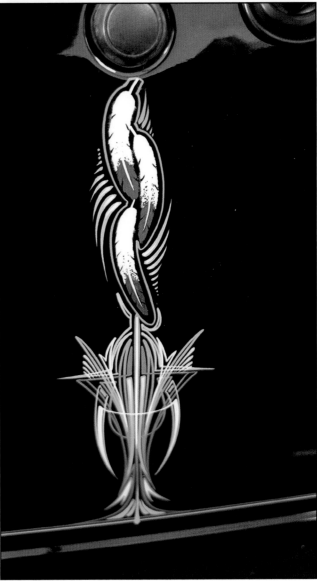

ROD Powell

SUPPLIES:

Paint Media: 1-Shot® lettering enamels and House of Kolor® shimrin bases

Brushes: #00 Xcaliber striping brushes, Jenson's Swirly-Q JS-2 brush, Winsor Newton Brush

Other: 3M™ No. 233 ⅛-inch tape, Electro Pounce, wax and grease remover, Xcaliber brush preservative

I was born in 1940 in Salinas, California. Growing up, my father would take me to the Salinas Drags and car shows. I bought car magazines and read about Von Dutch, Dean Jefferies, and Larry Watson. I first tried striping on the dash of my dad's Hudson Hornet with watercolor brushes and poster paint. Next, I tried model car enamels. That was a little better, but I still didn't know where to get a striping brush.

One day while at the Monterey Kar Kapades Show, I saw Dean Jefferies striping. He was painting weird cartoons all over the dashboard and package tray. Shortly after that, Don Varner moved to Salinas and I got to hang out and watch him paint and stripe. I began to learn about lacquer paint, kandy toners, 3M 1/4-inch tape, Mack brushes and 1-Shot® striping enamel.

After graduation I worked in body shops and did custom paint work at night in the college shop classes and in my garage. I built a radical chopped Merc and painted it kandy tangerine flake. It won sweepstakes at the Oakland Roadster Show. All of my cars were lowered and custom-painted. They were my rolling advertisements.

A few years later Andy Southard, a well-known pinstriper and photographer from New York, moved to Salinas. Watching him I learned more about striping techniques: how to hold the brush, palette the paint and pull longer lines. We became good friends and he striped many of my paint jobs. Thanks to Andy's photographs, the cars I worked on began to get recognition in magazines.

In 1969, I decided to go into business for myself and opened Custom Paint Studio. The shop became well-known for the team of talented employees that worked with me through the years. We built cars for Bob Larivee's ISCA show circuit and flamed hot rods for Tom Prufer. Our work won awards in all of the shows.

In 1971 I hosted a picnic-barbeque-car-run for my friends and customers in a local park that eventually grew into an outdoor show that filled the Monterey Fairgrounds. As the show grew, we started an open house at my shop where my painter friends made signs and awards for the next day's event. We also striped any cars that needed a finishing touch. Our honored guest list included such names as George Barris and Ed Roth.

After 25 years I decided to take a break. I closed the shop and ended the car show. I still have a shop in Salinas where I stripe and do other custom paint projects. I specialize in the traditional striping and paint styles I grew up with and enjoy working with old friends and customers who like what I do.

Step 1

Step 2

Step 3

Step 4

Step 5

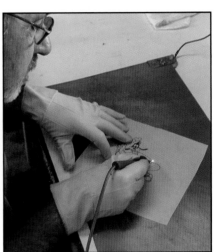

Step 6

Step 1:
The subject was a 15-gallon can painted with House of Kolor oriental blue kandy over a sparkly silver basecoat. The can had been topped by a few coats of urethane clear and was ready to decorate.

Step 2:
After cleaning the surface with wax and grease remover, I laid out the pattern using 1/8-inch masking tape. I began by taping a centerline on the front of the can, using it as a starting point. I left an open area on the upper front to add some cartoons and striping designs.

Step 3:
I overlaid the finished tape design with strips of wider 3M No. 233, and two-inch masking tape. Then I pressed the tape as flat and smooth as possible so the impression of the 1/8-inch tape line was visible. With a sharp X-Acto knife, I cut through the two-inch tape, staying close to the center of the 1/8-inch tape impression, and made sure I didn't cut through the bottom layer into the paint.

Step 4:
The flames were painted with a fade of House of Kolor's white base, chrome yellow, and tangelo orange. Two more coats of urethane clear were applied with a light touch of a yellow-gold dry pearl for an extra highlight. When the clear was dry, I removed the tape and smoothed the edges. Rough spots were lightly wet-sanded with 1500-grit sandpaper. I cleaned the can again to prepare for striping and artwork.

Step 5:
I created a sketch of the cartoon character, and transferred it to a sheet of medium-weight transfer paper.

Step 6:
For the pounce pattern, I laid the sketch onto a piece of sheet metal connected to an Electro-Pounce. I traced over the drawing with the stylus, burning a series of tiny holes into the paper, and wearing gloves to protect myself against an electrical shock.

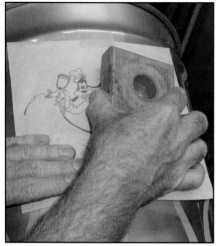

Step 7

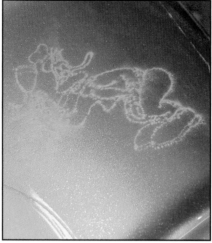

Step 8

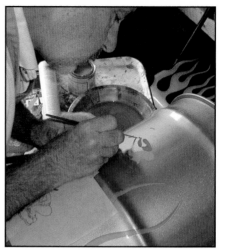

Step 9

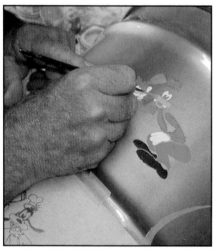

Step 10

Step 11

Step 12

Step 7:
I applied the pattern to the area left empty earlier and secured it with a few small pieces of tape. I transferred the pattern by lightly tapping and rubbing across the paper, using a pounce pad filled with blue chalk. This forces the chalk through the holes in the paper.

Step 8:
When the pattern was lifted, a chalk outline remained but it was messy. I gently blew away the excess chalk, and a faint outline of dots was left as a guide for the paint work. If you blow too hard and it disappears, simply wipe it off and reapply the design.

Step 9:
I began filling in the pattern, starting with the larger, less detailed areas first. I used a Winsor Newton brush to fill in as much of the color as possible, leaving a small amount of space along the edges for the black outlines. I taped the pattern sketch near the work area for reference in case I accidentally filled in too much, or smeared the chalk line.

Step 10:
Now I started adding the smaller details. The eyes, teeth and gloves were polar white and the shoes were medium brown. A paint gun was also added using silver.

Step 11:
When the figure was filled in, I added a heavy black outline to separate the colors, using a silver white Script brush. The outline added the classic cartoon look the customer craved.

Step 12:
To outline the flames, I chose to use a bright lime green. I mixed the color in a small plastic cup from Mr. J's, with a stir stick from Starbucks. The Jackson Pollock tray acted as a portable workspace.

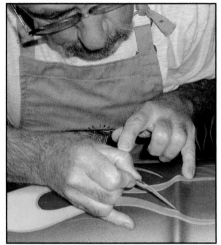

Step 13

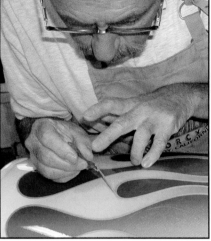

Step 14

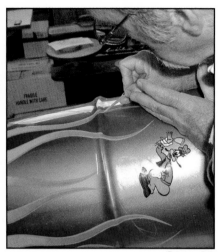

Step 15

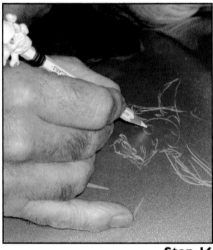

Step 16

Step 17

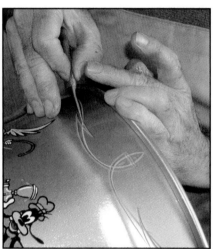

Step 18

Step 13:

For this stripe I used an Xcaliber 00 brush. The bumps can be troublesome so I flipped the brush upside down to keep a more consistent line through the concave area, steadying my painting hand with my free hand. Then I flipped the brush back over the right way. Next, I tied it into the rest of the line and continued striping.

Step 14:

As I approached the teardrop areas of the flames, I lifted my hands slightly while twisting the brush between my fingers. The brush rotated as I pulled through the curves and almost ended up backward. This method keeps the brush from flipping to the side and causing jagged or irregular stripes.

Step 15:

To finish off the ends of the flames, I reversed position and stepped to the opposite end of the can. Now I can pull the brush into the tip, lifting it off the surface near the end to get a nicely tapered point.

Step 16:

Another favorite character of the customer's was the flying eyeball. I added a couple to the design by first sketching directly on the can with a white Stabilo pencil. The pencils are water-soluble, so I was able to wipe them off with a damp cloth after the brushwork was finished. If you are clear-coating your work, be sure to clean off the pencil lines with a 3M white scuff pad, with Ajax and water, or the lines may show up through the clear.

Step 17:

I then filled them with color following the same steps I did for the Goofy cartoon, and outlined them in black.

Step 18:

I did some simple striping around the top band of the can, which was left open for this purpose. I used the rib around the can as a guide and balanced the brush without the support of my left hand.

Step 19   **Step 20**

Step 19:

The striping brush in the picture was a good place to add some scroll striping with a Jenson's Swirly Q JS-2 brush. I added my signature at the end of the line to finish this side of the can.

Step 20:

The striping tied things together. I cleaned up any smear or stray paint with a bit of Meguiar's No.7 Show Car Glaze, a pure polish, and a very soft cloth. Any stubborn spots were removed with Meguiar's No. 2 fine-cut cleaner.

The Finished Piece:

The colors are bright and should look great in a hobby room. A lid or cover can transform the can into a small table or lamp stand.

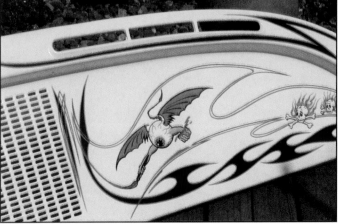

BLAINE Scott

SUPPLIES:

Paint Media: 1-Shot® Lettering Enamels
Brushes: Mack 000
Other: Terpinoid, mineral spirits, Stabilo Pencils, $\frac{1}{2}$-inch masking tape, razor blade, unwaxed Dixie cups wooden ruler, wax & grease remover, Windex

Like many kids of the post-World War II era, Blaine Scott was influenced by the unavoidable connection between planes and cars. This experience led to the boom in the custom-car culture as artists embraced the freedom to modify otherwise utilitarian objects. By erecting models and carefully executing the finishing details, Scott began to understand his capabilities as an artist and feel his passion for the custom culture.

In 1964, Scott noticed a mild custom in a trade-in lot in Lawrence, Kansas, that had been striped by a sign-painter and pinstriper called King George II. King George was the go-to guy in the Midwest at the time, and was best known for his striping work with Daryl Starbird. King George would go on to introduce Blaine to airbrushing, pinstriping, and screenprinting. During the 1970s, Scott and his mentor hit the fair circuit, working in tandem to sell screenprinted iron-ons and airbrushed T-shirts.

Scott later moved to Kansas City, where he continued custom sign-painting and kept striping. During this time, Scott befriended local stripers John Freeman and John "Tiny" McTaggert. Freeman was an established striper who influenced Scott's technique. Scott spent five years working in McTaggert's sign shop, gaining much more knowledge. Scott then accepted Butch Tucker's invitation to stripe and study with him in Phoenix. Opportunities for striping jobs came from car dealers and hot-rod shops. As computers began to compete with human sign painters in the 1980s and 1990s, Scott turned to the car culture.

In Wichita, Scott was embraced by the growing custom-car community and was asked to head up the striping portion of Big Dog Motorcycles's graphics department. As the new company grew, so did Scott's crew. He now supervises three other stripers and continues to stripe anything and everything.

Step 1

Step 2

Step 3

Step 4

Step 5

Step 6

Step 1:
I wiped down the vinyl with mineral spirits to eradicate any oil or grease, and finished it off with Windex to eliminate static electricity. I-Shot® will stick, is flexible, and wears surprisingly well.

Step 2:
I used mineral spirits to clean out the oil in the brushes.

Step 3:
I squeezed out the spirits from the brush. Then, I thinned the paint with mineral spirits by adding a few drops at a time until I achieved the right workable consistency.

Important note:
You must add a hardener to I-Shot® when painting onto Naugahyde or similar material. Failing to catalyze the paint will result in a much-delayed dry time—by as much as three days.

Step 4:
I made reference points with a Stabilo pencil, letting the design evolve as I progressed.

Step 5:
I loaded and paletted the brush on an old magazine.

Step 6:
I started with a teardrop and built the design from there.

Step 7

Step 8

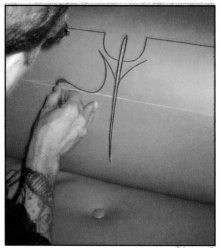

Step 9

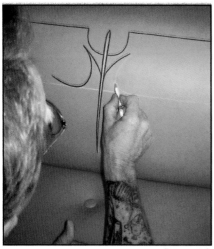

Step 10

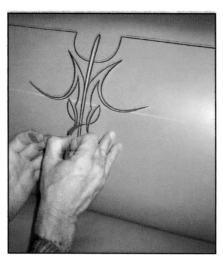

Step 11

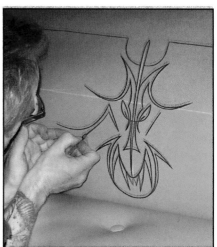

Step 12

Step 7:
Here I painted left to right, eyeballing the design to protect the symmetry.

Step 8:
I drew more lines, enough so that a scary face started developing.

Step 9:
I used the Stabilo guidelines to keep things even.

Step 10:
I striped the left part of the design. Using the Stabilo pencil gave me an idea as to where the right side should lay out

Step 11:
More drawn lines start to form the monster's eyes.

Step 12:
The basic face finished, I added more lines left to right.

Step 13

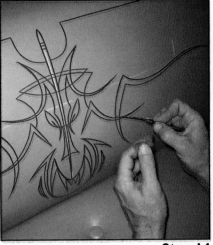

Step 14

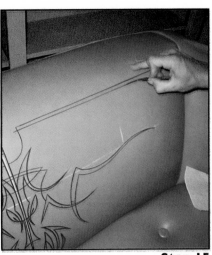

Step 15

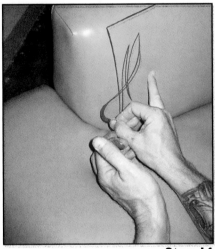

Step 16

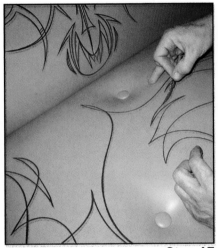

Step 17

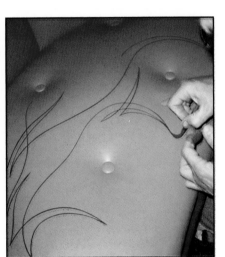

Step 18

Step 13:
I used the horizontal line to keep the long lines in order.

Step 14:
Now some finishing touches here and there.

Step 15:
More long lines to help frame everything.

Step 16:
I drew some swoops on the corners to finish off the back of the couch.

Step 17:
Here's the real fun part: On the seat, I just ripped crazy lines everywhere.

Step 18:
I finished it off with a nice little design and signed it. Ready for action!

Blaine Scott

JEFF "VON DAGO" Scozzaro

SUPPLIES:

Paint Media: 1-Shot® lettering enamels
Brushes: Mack striping brushes

You know you've made it when everyone seems to know your name. Jeff "Von Dago" Scozzaro's career spans more than 37 years. Highlights of his work include award-winning, one-off paint jobs and the inclusion of his work on magazine covers, in museums, and even a film documentary.

Jeff won his first award at age 10 for best paint in a competition sponsored by model-maker Revell. As a teenager, Dago experimented with paint on his friends' cars and motorcycles. In addition to learning on the job, Dago attended the esteemed Pasadena Art Center College of Design and graduated from Los Angeles Tech's Sign Painters Program. He started his own paint shop, aptly called Jeff's Place, in 1969.

Located in Anaheim, California, Jeff's Place afforded the ambitious Scozzaro a prime vantage point from which to view and impact the fertile SoCal scene. The client list at Jeff's Place was star-studded and extensive. Six of Jeff's creations have become Revell Company models, including the Redneck Power tow truck Billy Carter used at his Plains, Georgia gas station, and more than 45 of Jeff's customs have graced the covers of automotive magazines.

Now located in Hayden, Idaho, Jeff has built a local name for himself by striping and lettering the area's large community of hot rods and antiques. Although he signs Dago, his full moniker is Von Dago in homage to the legendary Von Dutch, who started the pinstriping culture in the 1940s and 1950s.

In 1996, he was nominated by his peers to become a member of the Route 66 Hall of Fame in San Bernardino, California. Also in 1996, Jeff became the 38th inductee of the Pinstripers Hall of Fame, in Jonesville, Michigan.

Major influences include Kenny Youngblood (whom he considers his mentor), Ron Lester (who gave him his very first Mack brush), Dave Whittle, Kim Dedic, Bob "Bobbo" Dunn, and last but certainly not least, Glen Weisgerber.

Step 1

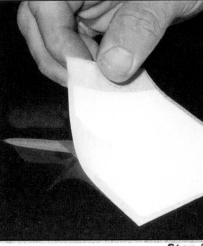

Step 2

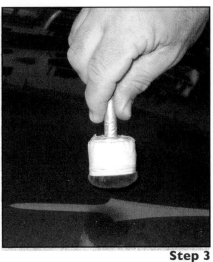

Step 3

Step 4

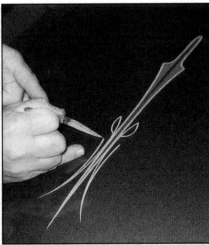

Step 5

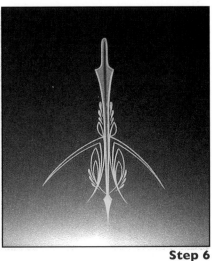

Step 6

Step 1:
I evenly applied 1-Shot® dry gold size with a few drops of 1-Shot tan to make it easier to see the size and to ensure proper coverage.

Step 2:
I applied 23-karat patent leaf by pressing the sheet onto the design. The excess leaf was removed by rubbing with a cotton ball.

Step 3:
Using a spinner tool with a velvet pad, I engine-turned the design using light pressure and a 50% overlap.

Step 4:
I pinstriped the center of the gold with a purple teardrop design.

Step 5:
I continued creating the design, giving it balance and more eye appeal.

Step 6:
Ba-Da-Bing! Total time to complete (not counting the hour dry-time for the gold size): a "whopping" 10 minutes.

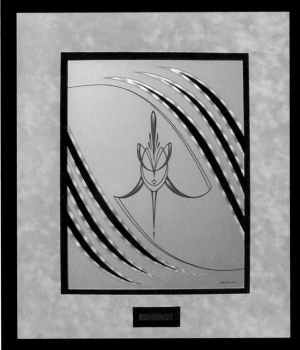

JEFF Styles

SUPPLIES:

Paint Media: 1-Shot® Lettering Enamel
Brushes: #0 Hanover Striping Brush, #4 lettering quills
Other: 1-Shot® hardener, Scotch-Brite pad, red variegated Gold Leaf, 3M™ masking tape, low-tack TransferRite masking paper, 1000-grit Sandpaper, PPG basecoats, PPG clearcoat

The year was 1980 and Jeff Styles was 13 years old. He had always enjoyed watching his father pinstripe and finally asked to be taught the artform. That day he was handed his first brush and given his first lesson in what would become his lifelong passion and profession.

Styles obsessively practiced and striped on anything he could get his hands on. One day, as crazy fate would dictate, Styles bumped into striping master Butch Tucker of Mesa, Arizona. He was on his way home from school when Tucker's 1956 Chevy wagon caught his eye. Simultaneously, Styles's striped bike caught Tucker's eye. A little intimidated, Styles was thrilled when Tucker began to teach him striping skills that he would never forget.

A flame specialist, Styles turned his hobby into a full-time job. Today he pinstripes for many of the dealerships and collision centers in Southern California, and immerses himself in custom paint jobs from start to finish.

The Project:

There comes a time when every striper needs a cool striping box, or in Jeff's case, a new one. For this project, Styles transformed his circa-1984 tool box into a veritable treasure trove by applying some cool ideas to an otherwise boring container.

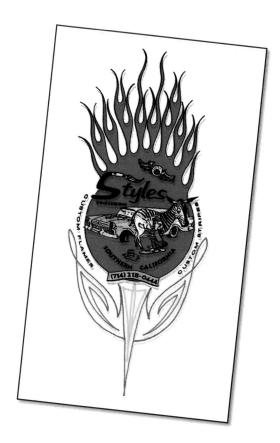

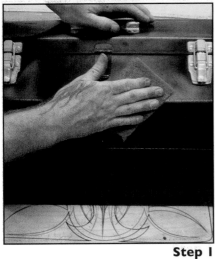

Step 1

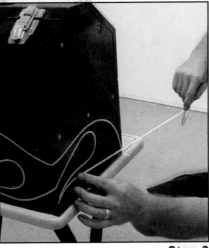

Step 2

Step 3

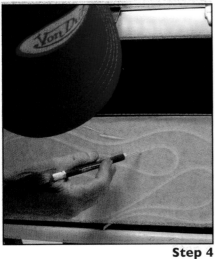

Step 4

Step 5

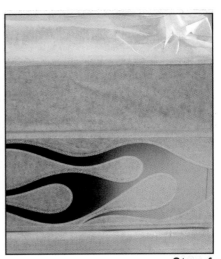

Step 6

Step 1:
Because I'm going to clearcoat this project in the end, I had to prep the box by sanding or scuffing with a gray (light-grit) Scotch-Brite pad. Be sure to mask off the clamps before sanding to prevent the chrome from getting scratched and covered with clear.

Step 2:
I laid out the flames using 3M™ eighth-inch tape.

Step 3:
To mask the design, I used a low-tack TransferRite paper, making sure to cover the entire flame job. Secure the paper down onto the design with a hard squeegee.

Step 4:
The tricky part is cutting out the flames. Beginners should be careful at this step. I use a very sharp blade, and apply very little pressure. If you press too hard, you'll cut into the basecoat.

Step 5:
I peeled off the part to be painted. Here's where I get a good sense of how the design will look.

Step 6:
I began by airbrushing and establishing a PPG solid white basecoat as a foundation for subsequent colors. This step is a must when painting on black or dark surfaces.

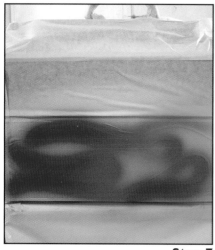
Step 7

Step 8

Step 9

Step 10

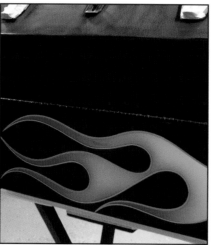
Step 11

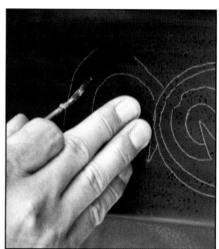
Step 12

Step 7:
The colors are up to you. I wanted the flames to look lively while maintaining a traditional look, so I faded from yellow to orange, then airbrushed red into the tips.

Step 8:
Because it peels off in one piece, the low-tack TransferRite paper saves a lot of time and headaches.

Step 9:
With the flames completed, I applied a coat of clear and allowed it to dry overnight. I sanded the design elements flat using 1000-grit sandpaper. This protects the basecoat and eliminates the flames' edge.

Step 10:
Here's the moment I've waited for—the striping phase. I chose 1-Shot® lime green to outline the flames. 1-Shot® hardener was added to prevent wrinkling.

Step 11:
The lime green stripe looked great, but there was still a lot of blank space to fill up.

Step 12:
A pinstriper's box isn't complete without a tribute to Von Dutch, so I decided to add a flying eyeball with variegated gold leaf wings. I used Saral paper to trace and transfer my design onto the box, and then applied gold-leaf sizing very carefully, with a Mack #6 lettering quill.

Step 13a

Step 13b

Step 13c

Step 14

Step 15

Step 16

Step 13:
After the gold size dried for about 30 minutes, I covered all areas with leaf, and then used a soft cloth to rub off the excess leaf. A great way to test for size readiness of variegated leaf is to lightly drag your knuckle across the size. To secure leaf firmly to the surface, place a sheet of paper over one leaf at a time and rub a squeegee across it without sliding. This step removes wrinkles.

Note: *Automotive Gold Leafing*, a DVD featuring Gary Jenson, is an excellent and comprehensive instruction on gold leafing.

Step 14:
The eyeball was filled in with white, and then green.

Step 15:
I airbrushed green in the lower half of the eyeball to create a shadow and to implement a 3-D effect.

Step 16:
As a final touch, I striped some veins on the eyeball.

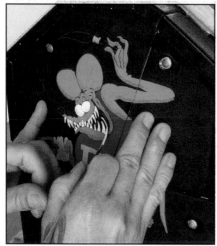

Step 17a

Step 17b

Step 18a

Step 18b

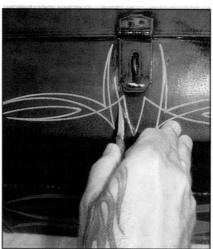

Step 19

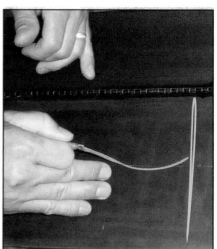

Step 20

Step 17a & b:
On the left side of the box, tribute is paid to another great legend, Ed "Big Daddy" Roth, with the addition of a "Rat Fink."

Step 18a & b:
"Lady Luck" was chosen to embellish the right side of the box. As with the previous designs, I filled in one color at a time.

Step 19:
A pinstriper's box isn't complete without some old-school stripes. I loaded my brush with 1-Shot® light blue to start the design. Add as many colors as you like.

Note: For multi-colored designs on a multi-sided project it is better to finish one color at a time than to finish one side at a time. Keep your brush loaded with the first color until you've finished each side, and then start with your next color.

Step 20:
On the back of the box, I continued with the light blue, and started a design in the center and worked from left to right.

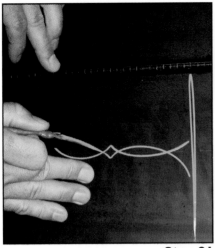

Step 21

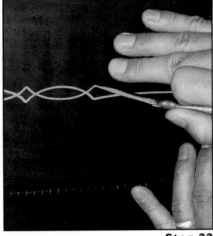

Step 22

Step 23

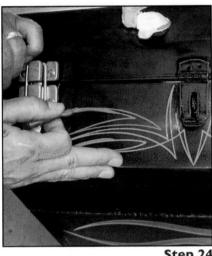

Step 24

Step 25

Step 26

Step 21:
I continued to build the design from Step 20.

Step 22:
I then moved on to the right, repeating the left side of the pattern.

Step 23:
For the next color, I chose a teal green, the same color used on the "Rat Fink" design.

Step 24:
I added the same teal green to the other design on the top of the box.

Step 25:
It seemed fitting to add an old-school striping design under the "Rat Fink."

Step 26:
I chose yellow as the second color and used it as a third color for the other designs on the box. Adding multiple colors to a design can add a helluva lot more punch.

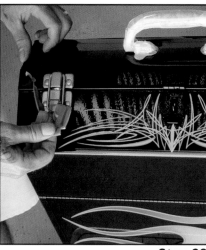

Step 27

Step 28

Step 27:
To achieve real depth and shine, I clearcoated the entire box.

Important Note:
To clearcoat 1-Shot®, you must add 10% hardener to the paint. Catalyzed 1-Shot® should be clearcoated within 15 minutes and three hours, or after 12 hours, of application. The time in between is the danger zone. The paint must be a little "green" (wet) or fully cross-linked (chemically dry) because you can't wrinkle stripes that are still somewhat wet, and you can't wrinkle them when the paint is fully dry either. The time in between is when the solvents can reactivate the paint, causing the stripes to wrinkle.

Step 28:
After all the masking was removed, I loaded the box with my striping enamels and brushes and off to work I went!

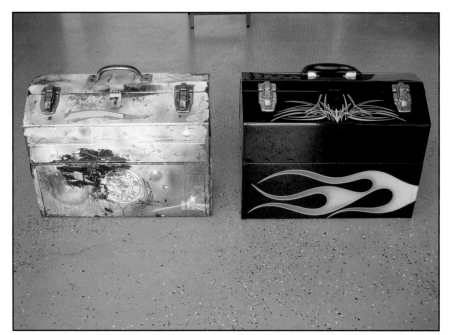

The Finished Piece:
Here's the comparison between my old striping box and the new one, which should last another 20 years.

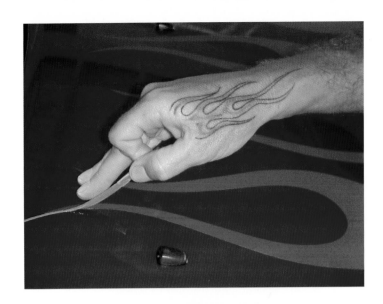

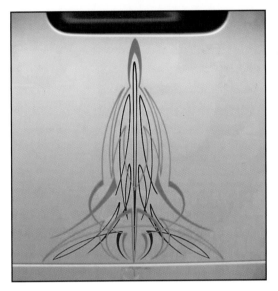

JOE Sulpy

SUPPLIES:

Paint Media: 1-Shot® lettering enamels
Brushes: An inexpensive one-inch brush, fineline brush, acid brush, and fine fan brush
Other: Chromabase burnt orange, Chromabase V7500 clear, 1-Shot® High Temp Reducer, printer's ink

Artistic talent has run in the Sulpy family in one form or another for 150 years. From the ornate decorations of Italy's churches to American folk art, every generation of the family has seen its share of true artists. Art was never forced on me but I have always had an artistic desire. I was a proficient enough drawer in high school to do renderings of my teachers and sell them for lunch money, which got me thrown out of school due to the artistic license I used in positioning the teachers in certain settings not popular with the school administration. As I recall, during the last conversation I had with the principal, I was told, "Mr. Sulpy your talents are obviously needed somewhere else."

In 1964 I was influenced by George Barris, Ed Roth, Gene Winfield, and Richard "Korkey" who, ironically, lived in my home town across the street from my school. I picked up my first brush in high school, more out of necessity than anything else. I couldn't afford to have someone else paint, letter, and do the graphics on my racecars. This forced me to teach myself the tricks of the trade.

After my racecars gained local notice, things began to snowball. I shifted gears and began designing, building, and painting custom cars. The custom van craze in the 1970s created a boom for business. It also afforded me a great experience and opportunity to further develop my own style.

After being in this field for more than 37 years on my own, I now rest my brushes at my son's custom shop in northwest New Jersey. Though I still pick up the torches every now and then, my true love is the creation and painting of murals, graphics, and pinstriping.

Step 1

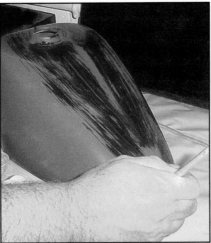

Step 2

Step 3

Step 4

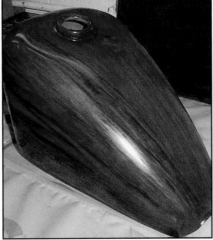

Step 5

Step 6

Step 1:
The tank was prepped and painted Chromabase orange.

Step 2:
I mixed 1-Shot® High Temp Reducer with printer's ink on the palette. (When using ink in wood graining a greater detail can be achieved due to the slower dry time.) I dry-brushed ink on the tank with a fine fan brush. (The same effect can be achieved using a wood graining tool or combs.) I covered the whole tank with dry-brushed ink.

Step 3:
Using a one-inch brush, I created a defined grain on the still-wet ink.

Step 4:
I used a coarse fan brush to add coarse grain.

Step 5:
I completed the graining process before the clear was applied. (Note that clear must cover all areas where ink is used.)

Step 6:
I masked off the tank for the flames.

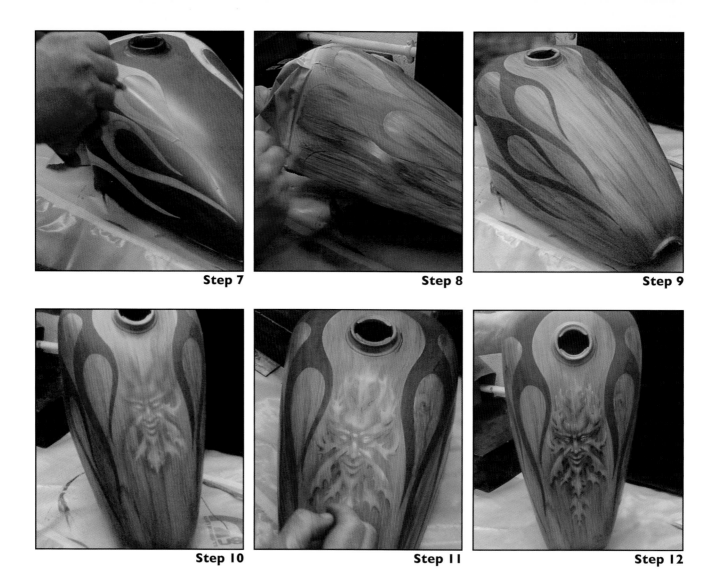

Step 7

Step 8

Step 9

Step 10

Step 11

Step 12

Step 7:
After cutting out the graphics, I airbrushed the remaining area.

Step 8:
I repeated the same steps to add wood grain to the newly painted area with 1-Shot® High Temp Reducer mixed with printer's ink.

Step 9:
After completing the graining of the graphic area, I removed the masking.

Step 10:
Next I airbrushed shadows and highlights for the start of the "Old Man Oak" graphic.

Step 11:
Then, I used a fine-line brush for highlights and lowlights. This created the most definition.

Step 12:
"Old Man Oak" is finished.

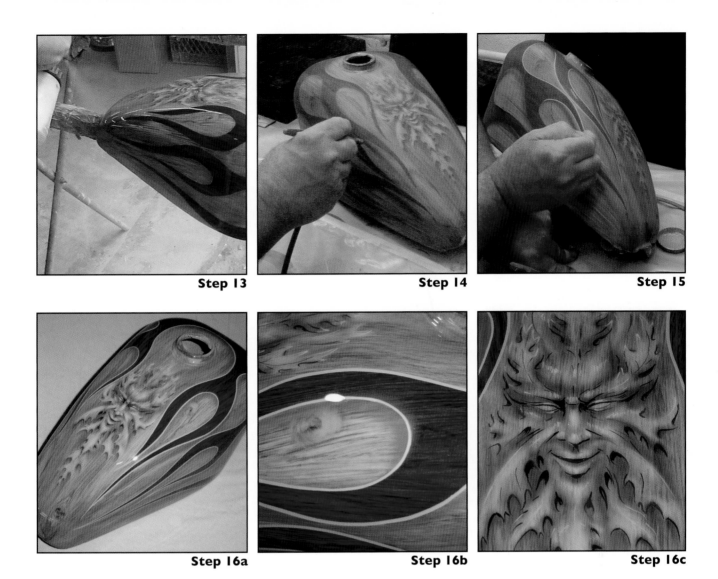

Step 13

Step 14

Step 15

Step 16a

Step 16b

Step 16c

Step 13:
Another mid coat of clear was applied to protect the wood and graphics.

Step 14:
After the tank was sanded with 1000-grit wet/dry sandpaper, drop shadows were airbrushed under the flames.

Step 15:
The tan base for the wood is an excellent contrasting color for outlining the red flames.

Step 16a, b & c:
After the striping was completed, two more coats of clear were applied, wet-sanded, and polished to a flawless finish.

Note:
A faux wood finish can be applied to just about any object or surface. Don't be afraid to experiment with different grains and color combinations.

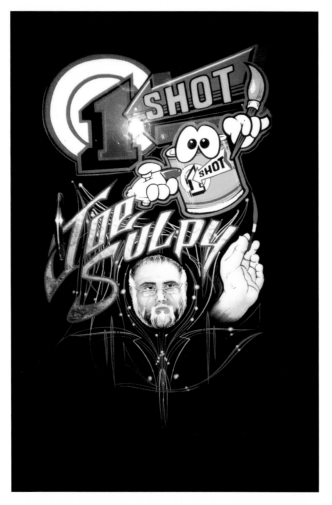

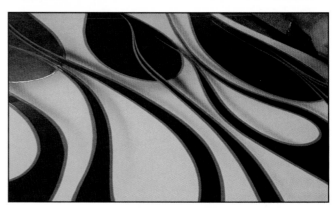

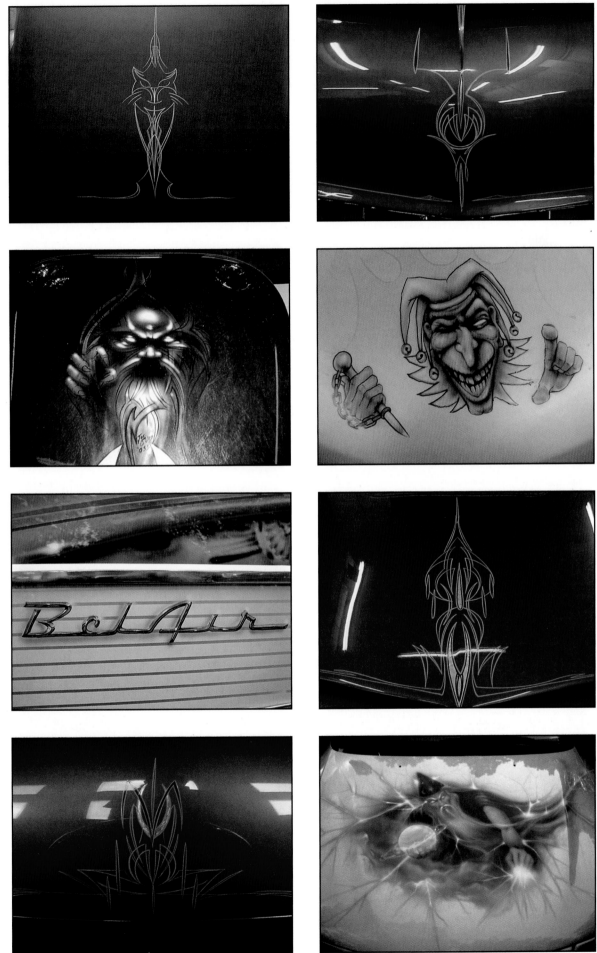

DALE Weber

SUPPLIES:
Paint Media: 1-Shot® lettering enamels
Brushes: Scharff 0 striping brush
Other: Wax & Grease Remover, 3M™ Fine Line tape,
    sponge

Like many in the custom car mecca of southern California, Dale Weber spent his youth soaking up the styles. By 12, he was poring over a Speedball lettering book trying to master Old English. He saved his lawn-mowing money to buy a whole set of steel calligraphy pens. Bill Dustin, a member of his church, owned a printing company and he kept Dale supplied with parchment paper and poster board to practice on.

Pen and ink led to brush and paint. He began to notice signs and show cards, and at 14 began painting signs for a small fashion store, spending hours to create a show card for which he could charge five or 10 dollars. He spent lots of free time doing calligraphy and illustration, but he realized it was the sign work that would sell. Business expanded to hardware stores and other shops.

Weber's interest in custom vehicles grew as he approached driving age. In high school he began pinstriping cars and lettering boats for friends and faculty (the handball courts were his first shop), while also working as a sign painter for Pay-Less Drugs. At West Valley Occupational Center in Woodland Hills for Sign Painting and Commercial Art, Weber finally learned about materials, layout, substrates and, yes, labor rates.

He admired many stripers in and around the San Fernando Valley: Walt Prey, Dino Hudlett, Jerry Dame, Bob Bond, Gary Berg, Larry Gloege and, of course, Von Dutch. Other influences included Tom Kelly, Mike Clines and Dean Jefferies.

When he was about 17, Weber met custom painter Paul Van Metre of Creations in Color. During the mid-1970s they collaborated on dozens of drag boats from all over the country—nitrocellulose lacquer and nitro methane fuel were a fabulous combination! In 1980, a year after marrying his better half, Ellen, Weber moved to Reno,

Nevada, to start from scratch. He's still there, painting signs and billboards, pinstriping race and show vehicles, and lettering trucks, sometimes for second-generation customers.

Weber has seen a lot of changes in the industry over the years—paint formulations, brush quality, availability, etc. None of those changes had as much influence on the industry as computers have, and while Dale uses his computer for some signwork and cutting masks for graphics, his pinstriping is done the old-fashioned way, by hand.

Weber says of his enduring love for the trade: "There are lots of sign stores in the Reno area that don't know a fitch from a quill or a dagger from a Beugler or sable from kazan or Smith's Cream from ice cream, but we still have a few brush slingers left to carry on the craft. Who knows, maybe my son Michael will be the next generation of Weber Graphics!"

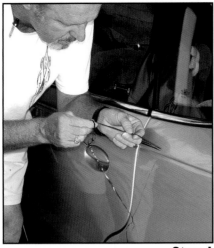

Step 1

Step 2

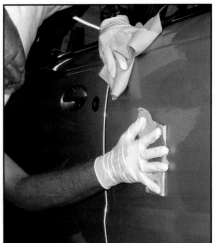

Step 3

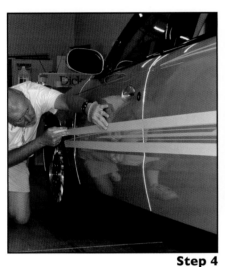

Step 4

Step 5

Step 6

Step 1:
I removed the existing tape stripes using a little heat to soften the tape enough to lift off without it breaking into little pieces. The remaining adhesive is eliminated with Rapid Remover and/or wax and grease remover.

Step 2:
This stuff stinks! A wad of linear acrylic polymers was successfully removed from the patient.

Step 3:
I always start with a clean, wax-free surface. Here I prepped the surface with Spies Hecker 7010 wax & silicone remover followed by PPG DX 103 Anti-Static Multi Prep (the Saturn panels were plastic and would have created static electricity unless treated).

Step 4:
I laid out the design with 3M™ fine line tape and masking tape. For this job, I could eyeball the proportions from side to side using the tape width as a visual guide.

Step 5:
The palette: several shades of mixed 1-Shot® purple were applied with a dog bone sponge. Three different tints of purple, with silver to ligh ten each progressive tint, were used.

Step 6:
Starting with the lightest shade of purple, I applied the paint with a sponge fading into the vehicle color by quickly dabbing in a slow progression with light pressure in one direction. The next deeper shade was blended into the first, followed by the blending of the darkest shade. To achieve seamless blends, always add layers "wet-on-wet."

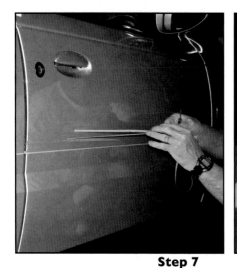

Step 7

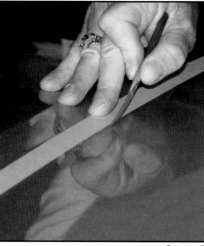

Step 8

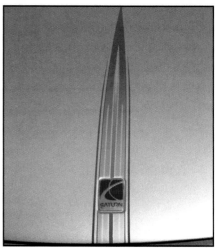

Step 9a

Step 9b

Step 10

Step 7:

I removed the tape while the paint was still wet. This is a very important step because if you allow the color to dry, you're likely to pull up some of the paint with the tape. Also, the paint edges level out better when the tape is removed while the paint is wet.

Step 8:

I pulled the pinstripes with a size 0 Scharff striping brush (made in England). You can use a half-inch to three-quarters-inch masking tape as a visual guide for straight stripes. For tight turns and easier bending, use one-eighth to one-quarter-inch tape.

Step 9a & b:

Here's the finished job—subtle colors for an understated car: a combination of purples, teal and even a touch of lime green in the graphics.

Step 10:

This John Hancock is considerably larger than my usual signature. But hey, it's my wife's car. What's wrong with a little free advertising?

...Our Flag Was Still There...

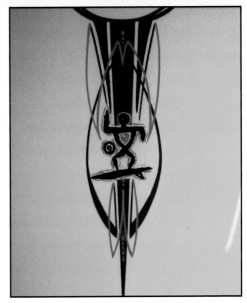

CLAY White

SUPPLIES:

Paint Media: 1-Shot® lettering enamels
Brushes: Grumbacher No. 1 and 00 brushes, Alan Johnson signature brushes, Mack striping brushes
Other: 3M™ No. 6306 fine-line paper, Iwata Eclipse HP-BCS airbrush, sponges

Clay White, a thoroughbred New Jerseyite, was born into a "car family" in 1948. His father, grandfather and uncles all had antique cars or racers. He started constructing models by age 6, and soon learned he was better at beautifying than building.

As a teenager there was plenty of local talent around. Stuff done by Les Dunham, Russ Mowry, and Russ Reber was everywhere, and it all looked good to White. But it wasn't until he watched Mowry gracefully letter his 1962 Corvette that he became truly hooked by the craft. While on leave midway through his stint in the military, White came home and was introduced to the dagger and quill by his friend, Jeff Cahill.

White didn't realize he could make a living striping and lettering until he attended the Bloomfield School of Sign Craft in 1975. By 1978, he was striping cars at night for dealerships. His first set of long straights took him more than two hours to complete, but he made more money striping that one car than he'd make in a full day of banging away in a body shop. White has been pulling long straights five days a week for more than two decades now, saving his weekends for custom work on bikes, street rods, and the like.

He relished the awakening of the Pinhead movement (although he wishes they had come up with a better moniker). Before then, stripers kept their trade secrets close to the vest, and with so little information being shared, lots of talents stagnated. He returned from his first Pinhead event in 1993 with a wealth of knowledge gained from the likes of Glen Weisgerber, Alan Johnson, Mr. J, and Joe Sulpy.

White's son Garett (White is married, with two children and three grandchildren) began working with his father during summer vacations. Now 32 and on his own, Garret's straights are barely distinguishable from his dad's.

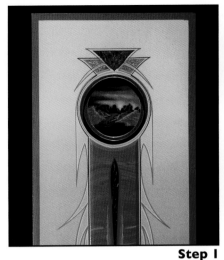

Step 1

Step 2

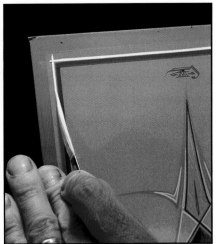

Step 3

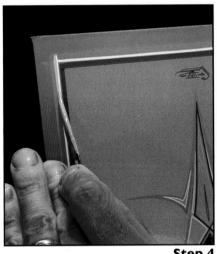

Step 4

Step 5

Step 6

Step 1:
For this project, I created a border that consists of a series of stacked straights on a finished piece. I started by masking the outer border, painting it, and letting it dry.

Step 2:
Using 3M™ fine-line tape, I laid out the approximate perimeter of the border. I calculated the number of colors I'd use and how thick each line would be in order to know where the border would end up.

Step 3:
Using a 00 Grumbacher brush, I pulled the first line as close to the tape as I could without touching it. The line should be slightly wide because it will be overlapped a little by the next line. When the first line is thinned out by the second line, the two will be the same width.

Step 4:
I repeated the process for the first line with subsequent colors. You can work wet or you can choose to let each line dry before starting the next. You can also run a little long on the corners, but try not to overlap too much as it can get a little sloppy toward the end. If a corner line extends too far, it can be removed with a paper towel that has a small amount of denatured alcohol on it.

Step 5:
I laid down the third color.

Step 6:
I chose black for the last line. The two most important lines were the inside edge of the first line and the entire last line. By saving the color from the initial border, I can clean up any mistakes made on the last line after everything is dry.

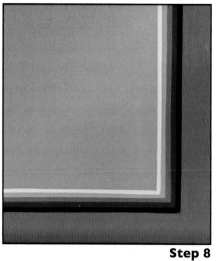

Step 7   **Step 8**

Step 7:
Here's the completed border with all of the straights aligned with the tape.

Step 8:
Here's a close-up of the border after the tape has been removed.

The Finished Piece:
Notice the nice, clean border of stacked straights.

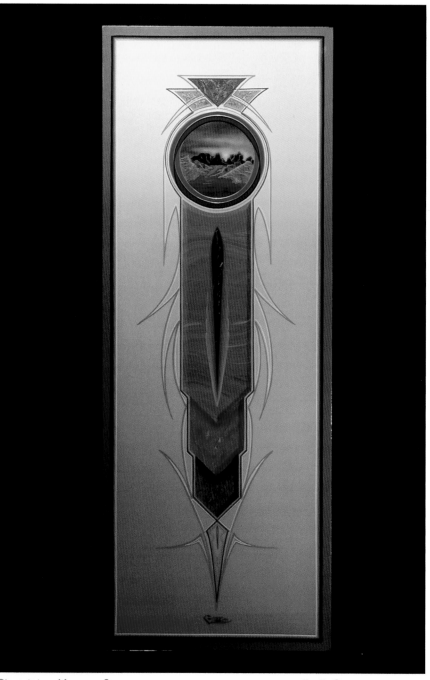

STACKIN' STRAIGHTS
by: Clay White

In 1985 I bought a new, bright red pickup truck for shop use. It needed some graphics, so I taped a six-inch wide belt-line panel that circumvented the body, sprayed it black with silver borders, and placed simple graphics to finish the front. I wanted to apply a one-and-a-half inch-wide blue neon stripe down the middle of the black section, but my airbrush skills were less than stellar and I knew I'd never pull it off with a spray gun.

At the time I had been doing long straights for dealers and had become quite proficient at it. I could pull a line better than I could spray one, so having more ambition than sense, I decided to mix up 13 shades of blue; from brilliant blue to robin's egg. Starting from the top and working my way down, I pulled long straights from dark to light and back to dark again. All lines touched, with no gaps—a total of 25 lines in a one-and-a-half-inch stripe. Twelve hours and countless aspirins later (for backache and eyestrain), the job was done and it was killer!

I haven't attempted anything quite so ambitious since, but I've found that stacking straights can be useful for adding depth to a border. It can also be used as a centerline on a design panel. OK, I can hear the snickers from here…how do you master straight lines? I wish there was some deep, dark secret to it, but there isn't. But there are three important factors to consider:

1. Use a good brush (I prefer the old black-handle Grumbacher).
2. Proper paint consistency (1-Shot® black).
3. A thoroughly loaded brush (palette the brush back and forth, probably two dozen times or more with a full load of paint to create what is essentially a controlled drip).

Other tips: I like to use 6306 3M™ fine line tape as a guide for my middle finger as I pull the line. Sixteenth-inch tape works best for me because it's not wide enough to drift back and forth across and has a very precise feel. Try not to labor too much when you pull a line.

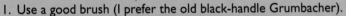

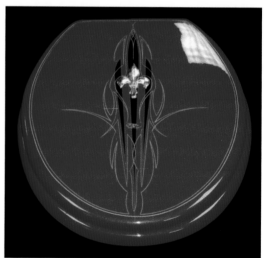

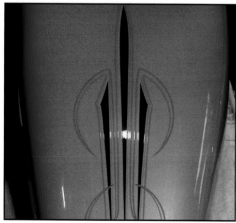

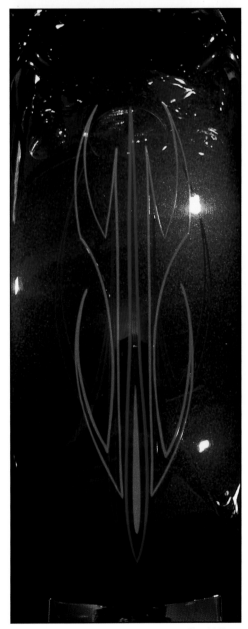

Index

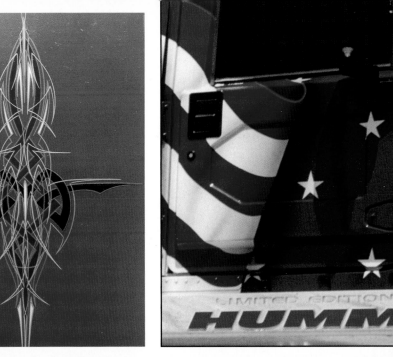

LIMITED EDITION **HUMM**

HOT ROD *Art*

Speedwa GRAPHICS
• VEHICLE LETTERING and GRAPHICS
• HAND PINSTRIPING • AIRBR
303•768•6880

THE ULTIMATE KUSTOM TRAINING
MASTER KUSTOM PAINTING IN 5 DAYS!
GET HANDS-ON TRAINING FROM WORLD-CLASS TALENT!
LAS VEGAS ■ CHARLOTTE, NC

1-DAY CLASSES

NEW! INTRO TO HOW TO KUSTOM PAINT MOTORCYCLES
This intro course is a terrific primer on the basics of airbrushing and the equipment and accessories needed to get started in motorcycle kustom painting. Robert Benedict's anatomy of an airbrush is a must!

INTRO TO AIRBRUSHING
Explore the different types of airbrushes, maintenance, air sources, safety issues, painting surfaces, preparation, and airbrush media.

INTRO TO PINSTRIPING
Recommended for those unfamiliar with pinstriping basics as a prerequisite to the 4-day Pinstriping Mastery class. You'll learn drills, techniques, materials & supplies, & much more!

INTRO TO AUTOMOTIVE GRAPHICS
Recommended for beginning airbrush users as a prerequisite to the 4-day Automotive Graphics class.

INTRO TO MURALS ON STEEL
Recommended for beginning airbrush users as a prerequisite to the 4-day Murals on Steel class.

OTHER CLASSES INCLUDE:
- T-Shirt Airbrushing
- Pin-Up Art

TUITION COSTS:
4-day classes – $575.
1-day classes – $150.
(Save $50 if you sign up for a 1-day & 4-day class)

4-DAY CLASSES

NEW! HOW TO KUSTOM PAINT MOTORCYCLES
Robert Benedict's cutting edge art and approach to kustom painting makes this one of the hottest new Getaway classes. With a special emphasis on the use of plotters and painting onto curved surfaces, this unique, progressive, and can't miss course is designed for the discriminating kustom painter with a hunger to reach the next level.

ACHIEVING PHOTOREALISM*
We're proud to offer Dru Blair's groundbreaking course that will reveal the secrets of painting photorealistic fire, ice, metal, water, glass, fur and many other subjects that often challenge artists.

CRAIG FRASER'S KUSTOM MASTER SERIES
Pro use of stencil systems, realistic flames, airbrush techniques, ground metal painting, & much more!

AUTOMOTIVE GRAPHICS
Learn the latest trends in auto kustom graphics, including flames, taping methods, complex designs, & much more from the star of T.V.'s *Trick My Truck*, Ryno!

AUTOMOTIVE MURALS ON STEEL
Kustom Masters Pantaleon, Cross-Eyed, Soto & gang guide you through a professional-caliber image featuring various texture f/x, color use with HOK urethanes, & much more.

PLEASE NOTE:
*The rate on the 4-day Photorealism class is $595.

- Advance your technical expertise
- Build your business
- Take advantage of networking opportunities

REGISTER NOW TOLL FREE
1-800-232-8998
INTERNATIONAL CALLERS 732-223-7878
Register Online www.airbrushaction.com
Sponsored by House of Kolor and Iwata

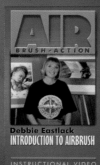